RANGER COLLEGE
MCMXXVI

Presented to

RANGER COLLEGE LIBRARY

By

CHRISTIAN SCIENCE COM. ON PUBLICATION

CHRISTIAN SCIENCE

CHRISTIAN SCIENCE

Its Encounter with American Culture

by

ROBERT PEEL

HENRY HOLT AND COMPANY

NEW YORK

ACKNOWLEDGMENTS

I am indebted to the Trustees under the Will of Mary Baker Eddy for permission to quote from the following works of Mrs. Eddy: *Science and Health with Key to the Scriptures, Miscellaneous Writings, Retrospection and Introspection, Unity of Good, No and Yes, Rudimental Divine Science, Christian Healing, Message to The Mother Church for 1901, The First Church of Christ, Scientist, and Miscellany.* Appreciation is extended to Longyear Foundation of Brookline, Massachusetts, for the privilege of quoting from some portions of the historical material in its collection. Grateful acknowledgment is also due the following publishers and individuals for permission to quote from the books and periodicals indicated:

Trustees of The Christian Science Publishing Society: for excerpts from *The Christian Science Monitor, Christian Science Sentinel, Editorial Comments on the Life and Work of Mary Baker Eddy,* and *The Life of Mary Baker Eddy* by Sibyl Wilbur.

Mrs. Frederic Wolsey Pratt and Odell Shepard: for selections from *The Journals of Bronson Alcott.*

Gerald Duckworth and Company, Limited: for excerpts from *The Resurrection Pattern* by Geoffrey Hoyland.

Charles Scribner's Sons: for extracts from *Character and Opinion in the United States* and *Interpretations of Poetry and Religion* by George Santayana.

Harper and Brothers: for excerpts from *America Set Free* by Count Hermann Keyserling and *The Dignity of Man* by Russell W. Davenport.

Longmans, Green and Company: for excerpts from *The Will to Believe* and *Pragmatism* by William James.

Houghton Mifflin Company: for excerpts from *The Education of Henry Adams* and *Shelburne Essays* by Paul Elmer More.

Abingdon Press: for an extract from *Psychology, Religion and Healing* by Leslie D. Weatherhead.

Science et Vie: for extracts from an article by E. Philipon, January, 1919.

New York *Times:* for an excerpt from an interview with Allan McLane Hamilton, August 24, 1907.

University of Chicago Press: for a letter by Will B. Davis in *The American Journal of Sociology,* September, 1954.

To my mother
Anne S. Peel
with deepest gratitude

The time has come when it is an urgent necessity that science should look at the pattern of life *as a whole,* taking every factor into account and excluding nothing from its inquiry. . . . Firstly, science must approach the problem in the spirit of relativity rather than of Newtonianism; it must look for patterns, with a readiness to recognize whole patterns, rather than for force-laws. It will no longer start with the presumption that certain events cannot happen, or must not happen, or ought not to happen, in the old force-law terminology; it will rather be content to ask simply whether the event did happen, or does happen, and if so, of what particular pattern it is the evidence. It will be on the look-out particularly for the evidence of faint patterns emerging into sudden prominence. . . . Relativity rules nothing out a priori; it is not concerned with rules, it observes patterns—and if it sees them it does not shut its eyes.

GEOFFREY HOYLAND: *The Resurrection Pattern*

PREFACE

This book records a neglected chapter of American intellectual history. It also explores an unrecognized potential in our contemporary spiritual resources.

I have centered my discussion on two persons, but the book is not about persons. The brief encounter between Amos Bronson Alcott and Mary Baker Eddy served to bring together two orders of ideas, related but distinct. The ideas take on flesh and blood when put in their historical setting, but the deeper purpose of this book is to disengage one of these orders of thinking from its extrinsic relations with the other, and examine its relevance to a distraught present and a future beyond human calculation.

The book had its genesis in a long-standing academic interest in New England Transcendentalism and an equally long-standing practical interest in Christian Science. Several years of graduate study at Harvard, and particularly work done under the guidance of Professors Perry Miller and Ralph Barton Perry, launched me on a consideration of the significance of the transcendental strain in American thought. Subsequently, years of active service in World War II and later as an editorial writer on *The Christian Science Monitor* deepened my conviction that Christian Science has a revolutionary contribution to make to contemporary society which is little recognized—even by many Christian Scientists.

To understand the failure of Transcendentalist theory and at the same time the success of Christian Science practice is to see both in a new light. The story of American Transcendentalism has been told many times; I gather up here only those aspects of it which explain its central promise and inevitable decay. The story of Christian Science, in terms of its cultural contribution, has not yet been written, though a valuable pioneer study is to be found in Henry W. Steiger's *Christian Science and Philosophy* (New York, Philosophical Library, 1948).

I have tried to be as objective as possible while stating with candor my own point of view. Complete objectivity in dealing with ideas is a myth, though a necessary ideal. The writer who approaches his subject from the "inside" has the advantage of knowing more about it from experience than the most sympathetic outsider can ever grasp through theory. If the present study falls somewhere between scholarship and journalism, it at least makes no pretense of treating exhaustively or definitively even the limited area of its concern. My purpose has been rather to open up new lines of useful exploration.

Some readers may feel that in the chapter entitled "The Pragmatic Test" I have paid insufficient attention to negative factors in the practice of Christian Science. I can only answer that this chapter is the merest sketch toward a reassessment of a vital subject on the basis of elements in it that are generally overlooked or misunderstood. It does not pretend to make the sort of methodical analysis characteristic of the denominational field studies being carried on, for instance, by the Department of Sociology at the University of Chicago under Everett C. Hughes; but it attempts to discover the dynamics of a movement which resists definition within current academic categories.

It should be emphasized strongly that the discussion of Christian Science in this book is in no way an "official" presentation. Despite my affiliation with the Christian Science Church, the book must stand or fall as one individual's independent view of a complex, controversial area of thought, presented with all the intellectual integrity and spiritual humility of which I feel myself capable.

I have omitted any consideration of the earlier encounter of Mrs. Eddy with P. P. Quimby as irrelevant to the purpose of this book, which is not biographical. Mrs. Eddy enters the discussion only with the publication of *Science and Health* in 1875, when her system of thought had taken essentially its present form, marked with the unmistakable impress of her own religious vision. Quimby's son, George, a staunch champion of his father, in later life wrote of Mrs. Eddy: "The *religion* which she teaches certainly *is hers*, for which I cannot be too thankful; for I should be loath to go down to my grave feeling that my father was in any way connected with 'Christian Science.'" And one of her severest (though most distinguished) critics, H. A. L. Fisher, has written: "When we ask what was the inner source of her power, the answer can only be that it was religion. . . . What exactly her book owes to Quimby remains, and will probably continue to remain, a matter of doubt: nor does it much signify. . . . Quimby would certainly never have written *Science and Health;* and in the development of Christian Science that book, and that book only, has been of decisive importance."

It may be thought a more serious omission that I have not considered the relationship of Christian Science to Hegelianism, since elaborate charges have been made that Mrs. Eddy "stole" her basic ideas from Hegel. Again, however, the question is too large to be considered in the present context, nor does it enter directly into the subject under discussion. For Hegel played very little part in the development of New England Transcendentalism; his influence on American thought came later, largely through the St. Louis school. But even if a Hegelian "influence" on Mrs. Eddy's thought could be established—and the recent study *Ordeal by Concordance* by Conrad H. Moehlman (New York, Longmans, Green & Co., 1955) amply demonstrates the fraudulence of the document on which the claim is based—it would hardly affect the conclusions of the present study, which is concerned with what Christian Science is, rather than how it came into being. Mrs. Eddy with some justice described *Science and Health* as "hopelessly original," and the phrase may be extended to her finished system as a whole.

It may be felt that I have quoted excessively in presenting my subject, but my aim has been to let the source material speak for itself wherever possible, and it has seemed best not to incorporate it into my own running narrative in the manner made popular by Van Wyck Brooks. In order to reduce the pedantry of footnotes to a minimum, however, I have not given references for quotations where the sources are obvious and easily accessible. In the case of Mrs. Eddy's works, any quoted passage may be traced to its source in a few minutes by reference to the published concordances to her complete writings. Her distinctive system of capitalization has been followed meticulously in my own discussions of Christian Science.

In presenting this subject, I have tried to strike a reasonable balance between the needs of the general reader and those of the academic student. There are, however, certain terminological difficulties which require explanation. The student of philosophy or theology will find that in Christian Science the words "individual" and "personal," respectively, are given different values from those which are ordinarily attached to them, individual signifying that which is unique to one's eternal, God-given identity, personal that which derives from the temporal and accidental and which separates one from the rich totality of being. The student of Christian Science, on the other hand, will find that the words "understanding" and "reason" as used by the Transcendentalists mean exactly the opposite of what he expects, for reason (*Vernunft*) is closer to what he means by "spiritual understanding," while understanding (*Verstand*) approaches what he means by "human reason."

I owe much to the several friends whose comments and criticisms helped me to solve some of the problems of communication presented by the theme of this book.

CONTENTS

CHAPTER ONE

THE PROPHETIC
SPIRIT

Science will be full of life, as nature is full of God. She will wring from her locks the dew which was gathered in the wilderness. . . . The time is not far distant. The cock has crowed. I hear the distant lowing of the cattle which are grazing on the mountains. "Watchman, what of the night? Watchman, what of the night? The watchman saith, The morning cometh."

—SAMPSON REED: *Oration on Genius* (1821)

I look for the hour when that supreme Beauty which ravished the souls of those eastern men, and chiefly of those Hebrews, and through their lips spoke oracles to all time, shall speak in the West also. The Hebrew and Greek scriptures contain immortal sentences, that have been bread of life to millions. But they have no epical integrity; are fragmentary; are not shown in their order to the intellect. I look for the new Teacher that shall follow so far those shining laws that he shall see them come full circle; shall see their rounding complete grace; shall see the world to be the mirror of the soul; shall see the identity of the law of gravitation with purity of heart; and shall show that the Ought, that Duty, is one thing with Science, with Beauty, and with Joy.

—RALPH WALDO EMERSON:
Divinity School Address (1838)

T HERE WAS A SPIRIT OF PROPHECY abroad in the land. Even before the Pilgrims set forth for the New World, their minister, John Robinson, had told them: "The Lord has more truth yet to break forth out of his holy Word.... I beseech you remember, it is an article of your church-covenant, that you be ready to receive whatever truth shall be made known to you."

Nevertheless, in the years and centuries that followed, Massachusetts orthodoxy had shown itself eminently unready to receive new revelations, and never was this truer than in

3

the period of which Emerson later wrote with wry exaggeration: "From 1790 to 1820 there was not a book, a speech, a conversation, or a thought in the State."

To be sure, an increasingly sterile Calvinism had begun to give way to a Unitarianism which promised the release of man's reason from oppressive dogmatism; but the new religion brought no quickening of the spirit, no warmth of the affections or the imagination, no dazzling revelation of unsuspected possibilities of being. Religion, indeed, became mere morality; faith became mere optimism; revelation, like miracles, was relegated to the past. God had spoken once through His Son, Jesus Christ, in a properly miraculous interruption of the natural order, but no conservative Boston Unitarian would dream of expecting anything now but cautious progress under the guidance of sound custom, received truth, rational morality, and commercial acumen.

It was on the face of these unpromising waters that the spirit of prophecy began to move about 1820. It started, as is well known, inside the fold of Unitarianism with William Ellery Channing. Never quite a Transcendentalist himself, the saintly and luminous Channing was to become the inspiration of many of the foremost Transcendentalists. Looking into the human heart, he found not total depravity but a natural loveliness which he felt to be the sign and proof of God's love. "The only God," he declared, "whom our thoughts can rest on, and our hearts can cling to, is the God whose image dwells in our own souls." A happy and good faith shines through his words, a childlike innocence ready to see the whole creation as a "birth and shining forth of the Divine Mind."

Looking forward to a radical advance across new frontiers of the spirit, he hailed the free mind "which does not content itself with a passive or hereditary faith, which opens itself to light whencesoever it may come, which receives new truth as an angel from heaven, which, whilst consulting others, inquires still more of the oracle within itself." And deeper even than the free mind he recognized the illimitably questing soul: "It thirsts continually for wider knowledge. It rushes forward to untried happiness. It has deep wants, which nothing limited can appease. Its true element and end is an unbounded good."

Here at last was the poetry of Unitarian faith, the appeal to the "oracle within," the large expectation of "new truth," the thirst for "wider knowledge" and "unbounded good," the confidence in a democracy of the spirit where each man might find in the depths of his own being the revelations of divinity. And slowly the vision found utterance in other quarters. Here, there, an ardent dreamer, a lonely thinker, a group of friends, a band of reformers, would be touched by the dawning spirit of the times and kindled to new assurances. By the next decade the flood of inspiration was sweeping sensitive and eager young New Englanders before it.

Influences poured in from the rest of the world—more especially Kant, Fichte, and Schelling from Germany, Cousin from France, Coleridge and Carlyle from Britain. To Locke, with his doctrine that all knowledge starts from sensation, the new movement opposed Plato, with his doctrine of the soul's innate ideas pre-existing in a realm of timeless, immaterial Being. Crowding Newton, with his mechanical universe running like a great clock, were to be found Plotinus and the later Neoplatonists, to whom matter was but the absence of God as darkness is the absence of light. And as Yankee clipper ships brought back the treasures of the East from China, so adventurous thinkers in New England rifled the sacred scriptures of the East in search of the eternal Brahma, serene behind the veil of *maya*, illusion, the fleeting sense-world of sin and sorrow and pain.

While the great ground swell of Jacksonian democracy was carrying America in far different directions from these, the Transcendentalists (as they were now being called) shared with the Jacksonians an ebullient faith in the individual, in boundless progress, in America itself. Moreover, though their mysticism might in some places oppose itself to the growing scientific spirit, more often it welcomed science with open arms, regarding nature as the language of deity, a perpetual revelation to the innocent heart and searching mind. From Swedenborg, whose "New Church" was winning distinguished converts in New England, they took the theory of "correspondences"—that every material phenomenon is but the symbol or counterpart of a spiritual reality.[1] This doctrine fitted well with the distinction between "understanding" and "reason" which they borrowed from the new German philosophers. The "understanding" (or lower faculty of intellect) busied itself with the facts of nature, using the methods of science; the "reason" (or higher faculty of intuition) alone could interpret these in the light of spiritual laws known to the Soul—by which they meant God Himself.

In 1836 the clarion call of the new faith was sounded, though it fell on the ear more like the lyric strains of a shepherd's pipe. In that year was published the small volume called *Nature*, in which Ralph Waldo Emerson set forth, at least by implication, all the important ideas that are to be found in his later works. The early dew still rests on this little book. It is the work of a young man, a rebel, for whom even the generous boundaries of Channing's Unitarianism were too confining. "Why should we look to the past at all for authority?" he asks. "The sun shines to-day also." The

---

[1] One of the outstanding Swedenborgians was Sampson Reed, whose *Oration on Genius* was delivered at Harvard in the year in which Emerson was graduated from that institution and in which Mary Baker Eddy was born in neighboring New Hampshire.

knowledge of man, as the schoolmen had said, is an evening knowledge, but that of God is a morning knowledge. Always before the Godlike vision stretch new and shining realms of unfolding creation. "There is more day to dawn," young Henry Thoreau was to declare in like spirit some years later. "The sun is but a morning star."

That was the mood of *Nature*. Revelation was a continuous instreaming power, not to be circumscribed by the already accomplished fact. Behind the fact or material appearance in every case lay the spiritual reality—lay broader relations, higher laws, unimagined potentialities. Might not the material world, indeed, be merely an image in thought? "Intellectual science," Emerson pointed out, "has been observed to beget invariably a doubt of the existence of matter," and he quoted the statement of Turgot, "He that has never doubted the existence of matter, may be assured he has no aptitude for metaphysical inquiries." Might not this brute nature, which seems so solid and intractable to the unillumined senses, be in fact but a bodying forth through man of the indwelling Spirit—"a projection of God in the unconscious"?

Emerson did not pretend to give dogmatic answers—denied, indeed, all dogmatic answers—but his faith was strong that to the bold mind and the rapt heart the exact correspondences between matter and spirit, appearance and reality, would reveal themselves. "The reason why the world lacks unity," he wrote, "and lies broken and in heaps, is because man is disunited with himself. . . . But when a faithful thinker, resolute to detach every object from personal relations and see it in the light of thought, shall, at the same time, kindle science with the fire of the holiest affections, then will God go forth anew into the creation."

There was shrewd observation, hard thinking, even a conservative sense of limits to be found as a sort of submerged element in *Nature*, but it was overwhelmed by the radiant tides of expectancy that swept Emerson to the confident question: "Who can set bounds to the possibilities of man?"

That was the mood, too, of his epochal address the next year on "The American Scholar," which has often been called America's intellectual Declaration of Independence, with its faith in the Godlike individual who was to free the American genius from the slaveries of the past. "As the world was plastic and fluid in the hands of God," declared Emerson, "so it is ever to so much of his attributes as we bring to it. To ignorance and sin, it is flint. They adapt themselves to it as they may; but in proportion as a man has any thing in him divine, the firmament flows before him and takes his signet and form."

The idea was developed and given its most challenging religious expression in his address the following year to the Harvard Divinity School. To the orthodox of his day the speech was madness and blasphemy. For thirty years he was not invited to speak at Harvard again. His words about Jesus in this speech are even today an affront to religious orthodoxy, though to modern agnosticism they speak of an almost forgotten faith:

> Jesus Christ belonged to the true race of prophets. He saw with open eye the mystery of the soul. . . . Alone in all history he estimated the greatness of man. One man was true to what is in you and me. He saw that God incarnates himself in man, and evermore goes forth anew to take possession of His World. He said, in this jubilee of sublime emotion, "I am divine. Through me, God acts; through me, speaks. Would you see God, see me; or see thee, when thou also thinkest as I now think."

Here was something Massachusetts had never dreamed to see: a young man telling his contemporaries that they could be what Jesus had been, do what he had done. Was this merely presumptuous infidelity outreaching itself or loftiest inspiration speaking in a new tongue? Calmly Emerson continued:

Historical Christianity has fallen into the error that corrupts all attempts to communicate religion. As it appears to us, and as it has appeared for ages, it is not the doctrine of the soul, but an exaggeration of the personal, the positive, the ritual. It has dwelt, it dwells, with noxious exaggeration about the *person* of Jesus. The soul knows no persons. It invites every man to expand to the full circle of the universe.

Again, after pointing out that Jesus, despite his respect for Moses and the prophets, did not hesitate to subordinate their initial revelations "to the hour and the man that now is; to the eternal revelation in the heart," Emerson added coolly that "it is my duty to say to you that the need was never greater of new revelation than now." A true teacher must show men "that God is, not was; that He speaketh, not spake."

This was heady wine for young seekers who were already imbibing copious draughts of romantic idealism from a dozen other quarters. And it was reinforced by noble words and daring examples from others in Emerson's circle. George Ripley, pastor of the Purchase Street Church, wrote to his congregation a manifesto of faith which was in effect a letter of resignation. In it he frankly acknowledged himself a Transcendentalist, almost as a minister today might announce from the pulpit that he was a Communist.

Even more startling to conventional Boston was Theodore Parker's eloquent ordination sermon on "The Transient and the Permanent in Christianity," which resulted in the virtual ostracism of the great preacher by his more respectable townsmen. Steeped in the new German Biblical criticism and fired with the new American spirit of revolt, Parker challenged the most sacrosanct doctrines of historic Christianity, questioned the authenticity and inspiration of much of the Bible itself, and declared heretically that ". . . it is not so much by the Christ who lived so blameless and beautiful eighteen centuries ago that we are saved directly, but by the Christ we form in our hearts and live out in our daily lives that we save ourselves, God working with us both to will and to do." Here was an American echo of the Straussian distinction between the historic Jesus and the eternal Christ. Jesus himself had set no bounds to the truth but declared, "I have many things to say unto you, but ye cannot bear them now. . . . Greater works than these shall ye do." And Parker concluded:

Let then the transient pass, fleet as it will, and may God send us some new manifestation of the Christian faith, that shall stir men's hearts as they were never stirred; some new word, which shall teach us what we are, and renew us all in the image of God; some better life, that shall fulfil the Hebrew prophecy, and pour out the spirit of God on young men and maidens; which shall realize the word of Christ and give us the Comforter, who shall reveal all needed things! There are Simeons enough in the cottages and churches of New England, plain men and pious women, who wait for the consolation, and would die in gladness if their expiring breath could stir quicker the wings that bear him on. There are men enough, sick and "bowed down, in no wise able to lift up themselves," who would be healed could they kiss the hand of their Saviour, or touch but the hem of his garment,—men who look up and are not fed, because they ask bread from heaven and water from the rock, not traditions or fancies, Jewish or heathen, or new or old; men enough who, with throbbing hearts, pray for the spirit of healing to come upon the waters, which other than angels have long kept in trouble; men enough who have lain long time sick of theology, nothing bettered by many physicians, and are now dead, too dead to bury their dead, who would come out of their graves at the glad tidings. God send us a real religious life, which shall pluck blindness out of the heart.

This was powerful and moving; but in such an atmosphere of restless expectation, where every misty-minded idealist was encouraged to prefer the "oracle within" to the vision or the Scriptures of the past, it is not surprising that a burst of noisy revelations filled the air. Around the golden group of Transcendentalists centered on Emerson were other strange and lonely figures, wrapt in private communion with the Soul of the universe; still others strode in on society like Amos or Hosea, demanding moral or civil reform in words full of Biblical fire; beyond them a rabble of visionaries proclaimed every sort of crusade and cause and revelation, like those disheveled bands of primitive prophets who came down to meet Saul "with a psaltery, and a tabret, and a pipe, and a harp."

Academic philosophy may deign to take notice of Emerson and a few other members of the "Transcendental Club" formed in 1836, at the suggestion of Dr. Channing, about the time *Nature* was published. But the transcendental ferment on the lower levels of intellect holds no interest for it. Far removed as New England Transcendentalism is from the intellectual rigors of Kant, the utopianism and religious enthusiasm at its periphery are completely beyond the bounds of intellectual respectability. Yet all this excitement suggests a powerful leaven deep at work in society, reaching even to those undistinguished levels where mesmerism, spiritualism, phrenology, and vegetarianism showed a restless people reaching out blindly for new sources of power, of assurance, of spiritual hygiene. The ferment may as easily be ascribed to the animal spirits of youthful democracy as to the workings of the Holy Spirit, to the disintegration of established religion as to the stirrings of a new humanitarianism, yet the surprising thing is the amount of genuine idealism and moral vitality to be found among these cranks and crusaders.

Brahmin Boston and Cambridge, in the person of James Russell Lowell, later commented on the spectacle:

Every possible form of intellectual and physical dyspepsia brought forth its gospel. . . . Everybody had a mission (with a capital M) to attend to everybody-else's business. No brain but had its private maggot, which must have found pitiably short commons sometimes. Not a few impecunious zealots abjured the use of money (unless earned by other people), professing to live on the internal revenues of the spirit. Some had an assurance of instant millennium as soon as hooks and eyes should be substituted for buttons. Communities were established where everything was common but common-sense. Men renounced their old gods, and hesitated only whether to bestow their furloughed allegiance on Thor or Budh. Conventions were held for every hitherto inconceivable purpose.

Frederick Henry Hedge, one of the leading members of the Transcendental Club, wrote with more sympathy in the midst of the ferment:

I am disposed to rejoice in these radical movements, which are everywhere springing up in the discontented spirits and misguided efforts of modern reform. Perfectionism, Grahamism, Nonresistance, and all the forms of ultraism, blind and headlong as they seem, have yet a meaning which, if it cannot command assent, must at least preclude contempt. They are the gropings of men who have waked too soon, while the rest of mankind are yet wrapt in sleep, and the new day still tarries in the East. The philosopher sees through these efforts, and knows that they are not the light that is to come; but he feels that they are sent to bear witness of the light, and hails them as the welcome tokens of approaching day. However our reason may disallow, however our taste may reject them, the thoughtful mind will perceive there the symptoms of a vitality which appears nowhere else. They are the life, however spasmodic, of this generation. There, or nowhere, beats the heart of the century.

Not since Ann Hutchinson had appealed to the Holy Ghost against the Massachusetts hierarchy, and the Quakers had introduced into the intellectual good order of Puritan theocracy their disturbing doctrine of the "inner light," had the centrifugal pull of private revelation so challenged religious authority. Yet the Puritan conscience continued to dominate the multitudinous ebullitions of the new spirit, the noblest theoretical expression of which is to be found among the Transcendentalists proper. Its most significant practical expression, on the other hand, is to be found in the antislavery movement. William Lloyd Garrison was still a Puritan when he wrote his famous words, "I am in earnest. I will not equivocate; I will not excuse; I will not retreat a single inch; and I WILL BE HEARD!"—and then proceeded to prove (as Henry Thoreau undertook to prove by very different means within the little world of Concord) that one with God makes a majority. For the moral idealism of an entire nation was rallied to the issue of antislavery before he was through, and history verified the words of the Unitarian minister, Samuel J. May, when he first heard Garrison speak: "That is a providential man; he is a prophet; he will shake our nation to its center, but he will shake slavery out of it."

Just as virtually all the leading Transcendentalists were eventually drawn into active sympathy with the abolitionist cause by their moral idealism, so Garrison was drawn by the spirit of the times into such indiscriminate enthusiasms as vegetarianism, women's rights, temperance reform, Sabbath reform, nonresistance, spiritualism, and the Perfectionism of John Humphrey Noyes. Of this last-named cult, one of Noyes' followers declared: "As the doctrine of temperance is total abstinence from alcoholic drinks, as the doctrine of antislavery is immediate abolition of human bondage, so the doctrine of Perfectionism is immediate and total cessation from sin."

In one way or another this millennial spirit pervaded the various group movements which sprang into exuberant being—Noyes' own Oneida Community, Robert Owen's New Harmony, the idyllic Brook Farm where Transcendentalists for a while almost proved they could live together, and a host of others. It flared out in conventions—like the Groton Convention of simple, shining-faced Come-outers from Cape Cod who rejected churches and sacraments and creeds ("All our meals are the Lord's Supper, if we eat with a right heart") and Millerites whose hearts burned for the second coming of Christ, which by their calculations was to take place in 1843. (It was at this convention that one young man announced: "Truth is Christ, and Christ Truth, and if we but knew all truth, this body would never die but be caught up and spiritualized.")

On a more "intellectual" level, but no less bizarre in character, was the Convention of Friends of Universal Reform which met at the Chardon Street Chapel in Boston for three separate three-day sessions during 1840–41. Emerson and Channing, Thoreau and Garrison, Parker and Lowell all attended, and Emerson's drawling account (bespeaking the level-headed Yankee even more than the open-minded Transcendentalist) has become the classic description of the yeastier aspect of that vivid period: "Madmen, madwomen, men with beards, Dunkers, Muggletonians, Come-outers, Groaners, Agrarians, Seventh-day Baptists, Quakers, Abolitionists, Calvinists, Unitarians and Philosophers,—all came successively to the top, and seized their moment, if not their hour, wherein to chide, or pray, or preach, or protest."

Not so well remembered is Emerson's comment on his

friend Amos Bronson Alcott in connection with this motley crew: "By no means the least value of this Convention, in our eye, was the scope it gave to the genius of Mr. Alcott, and not its least instructive lesson was the gradual but sure ascendency of his spirit, in spite of the incredulity and derision with which he is at first received, and in spite, we might add, of his own failures."

2.

That bustling nineteenth-century America should have produced a Bronson Alcott seems a piece of supreme irony. In Hindu society he would undoubtedly have been accounted a *mahatma*, a saint, by the many; eager disciples would have flocked to such a teacher to drink at the limpid wells of his serene and unworldly wisdom. But in the United States of America, already at that time judging success largely in extrovert terms, Alcott was a practical failure, a ludicrous misfit, the *reductio ad absurdum* of the Transcendental ethos. Even his most sympathetic admirers, even an Emerson, must sometimes laugh at his idiosyncrasies, or stand aghast at his terrible innocence, or grow bored with his stupefyingly single-minded pursuit of the ideal. He was, said Emerson, a "tedious archangel," and the phrase was just and has stuck. Yet again and again after talking with him the same Emerson would jot down in his journal such dazzled comments as these: "Wonderful is his vision. The steadiness and scope of his eye at once rebuke all before it, and we little men creep about ashamed." He could even call him "the most remarkable man and the highest genius of the time."

Nor was Emerson alone in his estimate. Thoreau, carefully choosing the words best calculated to outrage the bread-and-butter judgment of his countrymen, declared that Alcott was "the sanest man I ever knew." And Samuel J.

May, the Unitarian Abolitionist whose first impression of Garrison has already been quoted, wrote many years later of his earliest meeting with Alcott: "I have never, but in one instance, been so immediately taken possession of by any man I have ever met in life. He seemed to me a born sage and saint. He was radical in all matters of reform; went to the root of all things, especially the subjects of education, mental and moral culture."

Alcott was, in fact, the Schoolmaster of Transcendentalism—and a very radical schoolmaster indeed. His Temple School in Boston was one of the Transcendental scandals of the day, based as it was on the unusual Platonic doctrine of the pre-existence of the soul and the neglected Christian teaching (in regard to children) that "of such is the kingdom of God." The sharp-eyed Harriet Martineau in her *Society in America* held up to ridicule a schoolmaster "who presupposes his little pupils possessed of all truth in philosophy and morals, and that his business is to bring it out into expression, to help the outward life to conform to the inner light and especially to learn of these enlightened babes with all humility."

Alcott, in his experiments with child-centered education, was in one sense the father (or perhaps we should say the great-grandfather) of progressive education in America, but he was closer to the Wordsworth who addressed the child as:

> Thou best Philosopher, who yet dost keep
> Thy heritage, thou Eye among the blind . . .
> Mighty Prophet! Seer blest!

than to the John Dewey of *The School and Society* and *Democracy and Education*. Sensitiveness and common sense, as well as courage and audacity, marked many of his radical innovations in the classroom, but in his efforts to play Socratic midwife to the divine ideas inhering in the minds of his young pupils he relied on his own intuitive technique of "conversation" rather than on the more modern methodologies of "learning by doing."

It was the publication of his *Conversations with Children on the Gospels* in 1836 that was the undoing of the Temple School. Jesus, as well as Socrates, had taught by the question-and-answer method, and Alcott felt that by the same method children could be led, better than any adult, to a recognition of the translucent spirituality of the supreme Teacher, who had told his disciples: "Whosoever shall not receive the kingdom of God as a little child shall in no wise enter therein." After visiting one of the classroom conversations on the Gospel of John earlier in 1836, Emerson had written in his journal: "I felt strongly, as I watched the gradual dawn of thought upon the minds of all, that to truth is no age or season. It appears, or it does not appear; and when the child perceives it he is no more a child. Age, sex, are nothing. We are all alike before the great whole. Little Josiah Quincy, now six years, six months old, is a child having something wonderful and divine in him. He is a youthful prophet." And a week later he again recorded: "Mr. Alcott has been here with his Olympian dreams. He is a world-builder. Evermore he tries to solve the problem: Whence is the world? The point at which he prefers to begin is the mystery of the Birth of a Child."

His concept of birth was that of the "Ode on the Intimations of Immortality":

> Our birth is but a sleep and a forgetting:
> The soul that rises with us, our life's star,
>   Hath had elsewhere its setting,
>   And cometh from afar;
>   Not in entire forgetfulness,
>   And not in utter nakedness,
> But trailing clouds of glory do we come
>   From God, who is our home. . . .

But instead of the pessimism of Wordsworth, who saw the vision gradually fading into "the light of common day," Alcott possessed a boundless faith that the pre-existent glory could be kept alive through education, transforming men into the image of the ideal, reshaping society, opening up new possibilities of control over nature—and to this extent at least he shared with Dewey a dynamic concept of education as the handmaid of reform. Yet the full distance between the two men appears when we read these words from Alcott's introduction to the *Conversations with Children on the Gospels:*

Teachers must be men of genius. They must be men inspired. The Divine Idea of a Man must have been unfolded from their being, and be a living presence. Philosophers, and Sages, and Seers,—the only real men—must come as of old, to the holy vocation of unfolding human nature. Socrates, and Plato, and the Diviner Jesus, must be raised up to us, to breathe their wisdom and will into the genius of our era, to recast our institutions, remould our manners, and regenerate our men. Philosophy and religion, descending from the regions of cloudy speculation, must thus become denizens of our common earth, known among us as friends, and uttering their saving truths through the mouths of our little ones.

Shocked Boston, however, refused to be saved by the truths uttered by little Josiah Quincy and his fellows. Instead, it protested vigorously against the spectacle of six-year-old children discussing the mystery of birth, and in particular the Virgin Birth—delicately and reverently though Alcott handled these conversations. The Temple School dwindled to three pupils, then closed; and a brief successor came to an abrupt end in a storm of disapproval when it admitted a little Negro girl as a student.

Thereafter Alcott played schoolmaster to more mature

minds, and above all to Emerson, who never ceased to be fascinated by his extraordinary combination of the sublime and the ridiculous. In his now almost forgotten introduction to the *Conversations with Children on the Gospels* are to be found all the basic ideas to which Emerson gave more famous and lasting expression in his Divinity School Address a year or two later.[2] Alcott's own writing is deficient; his pen was never the equal of his tongue—though his "Orphic Sayings," whose "unintelligibility" caused his contemporaries such scornful mirth, offer no special difficulties to a generation familiar with Heidegger, Jung, and *Seven Types of Ambiguity*. Some of them, indeed, were quite simple: "The heart is the prophet of your soul, and ever fulfills her prophecies; reason is her historian; but for the prophecy the history would not be." And of the spiritual hero: "He is a creative element, and revises men, times, life itself. A new world pre-exists in his ideal."

The most eloquent expression of Alcott's vision is doubtless to be found in the rhapsodic climax of Emerson's *Nature*, in the passages attributed to an unnamed "Orphic poet." Here is the Neoplatonic doctrine of nature as the product of man's falling away from God, with the peculiarly activist twist given to it by Alcott, who held that as man reunites himself with his divine source and selfhood, not only will he read the symbolic language of nature aright but refashion that language to conform ever more closely to the divine Reality:

> Nature is not fixed but fluid. Spirit alters, moulds, makes it. The immobility or bruteness of nature is the absence of spirit; to pure spirit it is fluid, it is volatile, it is obedient. Every spirit builds itself a house, and beyond its house a world, and be-

---

[2] See Appendix A. I have included this introduction by Alcott, otherwise difficult of access for most readers, because of its prophetic interest in connection with the later appearance of Christian Science.

yond its world a heaven. Know then that the world exists for you. For you is the phenomenon perfect. What we are, that only can we see. . . . Build therefore your own world. As fast as you conform your life to the pure idea of your mind, that will unfold in great proportions. A correspondent revolution in things will attend the influx of the spirit. So fast will disagreeable appearances, swine, spiders, snakes, pests, mad-houses, prisons, enemies, vanish; they are temporary and shall be no more seen. The sordor and filths of nature, the sun shall dry up and the wind exhale. As when the summer comes from the south the snow-banks melt and the face of the earth becomes green before it, so shall the advancing spirit create its ornaments along its path and carry with it the beauty it visits and the song which enchants it; it shall draw beautiful faces, warm hearts, wise discourse, and heroic acts, around its way, until evil is no more seen. The kingdom of man over nature, which cometh not with observation,—a dominion such as now is beyond his dream of God,—he shall enter without more wonder than the blind man feels who is gradually restored to perfect sight.

No other thinker of the period aimed so high and speculated so daringly. Emerson found his friend's flights exhilarating, but for ordinary purposes retired discreetly from such dizzy heights to the lower plane of optimism about the world as it is, though with a quickened sense of possibilities beyond present calculation. Some of his Transcendental friends were unable to follow Alcott even as far as Emerson did. It is difficult, indeed, to find a satisfactory common denominator for all the group—ranging from the Plotinian Alcott to the strenuous Parker, with his "steel-cold intelligence" and his training in German metaphysics, who, in a conversation reported clinically by Emerson, "wound himself around Alcott like an anaconda; you could hear poor Alcott's bones crunch." They were all "idealists," but the term admits of vast differences in thought and temperament.

"Their leading idea," declared one of the ablest of them all, George Ripley, "is the supremacy of mind over matter," and the exaltation of mind and spirit runs through the period like a theme with endless variations. Even Abe Lincoln in Illinois, as remote geographically from Boston and Concord as he was intellectually from Alcott and Emerson, could write in the spirit of the times: "Happy day when—all appetites controlled, all passions subdued, all matter subjected—mind, all conquering mind, shall live and move, the monarch of the world."

At one end of the intellectual spectrum is James Freeman Clarke describing his Harvard education and early philosophical lessons in Locke: "But something within me revolted at all such attempts to explain soul out of sense, deducing mind from matter, or tracing the origin of ideas to nerves, vibrations, and vibratiuncles. So I concluded I had no taste for metaphysics and gave it up, until Coleridge showed me from Kant that though knowledge begins *with* experience it does not come *from* experience. Then I discovered that I was born a transcendentalist. . . ."

At the other end of the intellectual spectrum is nineteen-year-old Andrew Jackson Davis dictating, in a mesmeric trance, a stout volume published under the title *The Principles of Nature, Her Divine Revelations, and a Voice to Mankind*, in which the youthful clairvoyant stated: "The Universe must be united by a Living Spirit, to form, as a whole, ONE GRAND MAN. That spirit is the cause of its present form, and is the Disseminator of motion, life, sensation, and intelligence throughout all the ramifications of the One Grand Man." To this universal spirit the visible universe serves as a body: "Man is a part of the great Body of the Divine Mind. He is a gland or minute organ which performs specific functions, and receives life and animation from the interior moving Divine Principle."

This curious hodgepodge came from the intellectual back-woods of upstate New York and circulated in the humbler hinterlands of Transcendentalism in its later period of decline. But in the New Jerusalem itself, in the city of Boston, in the heyday of the new movement, Orestes A. Brownson had proclaimed a not wholly dissimilar doctrine, with something of the crude energy of a backwoodsman but with incomparably greater intellectual clarity, range, and sophistication:

> An intelligence which does not manifest itself, is a dead intelligence, a dead thought; but a dead thought, a dead intelligence, is inconceivable. To live, to exist, intelligence must manifest itself. God, being thought, intelligence in itself, must necessarily manifest himself. To manifest himself is to create, and his manifestation is creation. . . . But God can manifest only what is in himself. He is thought, intelligence itself. Consequently there is in creation nothing but thought, intelligence. In nature, as in humanity, the supreme Reason is manifested, and there, where we had fancied all was dead and without thought, we are now enabled to see all living and essentially intellectual. There is no dead matter, there are no fatal causes; nature is thought, and God is its personality. . . . This is not Pantheism. Pantheism considers the universe as God; but this presents God as the cause, and the universe as the effect.

This last contention was disputed in a very able attack on the Transcendentalists by James Murdock, who insisted that they were pantheists whether or not they admitted it, since they all held to but *one essence* or *one substance* in the universe. And to clinch his argument he quoted from an anonymous writer [3] in the "official" Transcendental organ, *The Dial*, who cheerfully equated pantheism with Transcen-

---

[3] According to a notation in Emerson's copy of *The Dial* in the Houghton Library, Harvard, the writer was William D. Wilson.

dentalism and gave this striking account of its theological implications:

Holding as they do but one essence of all things, which essence is God, Pantheists must deny the existence of essential evil. All evil is negative,—it is imperfection, non-growth. It is not essential, but modal. Of course there can be no such thing as hereditary sin,—a tendency positively sinful in the soul. Sin is not a wilful transgression of a righteous law, but the difficulty and obstruction which the Infinite meets with in entering into the finite. *Regeneration* is nothing but an ingress of God into the soul, before which sin disappears as darkness before the rising sun. Pantheists hold also to the *atonement,* or at-one-ment between the soul and God. This is strictly a unity of *oneness,* to be brought about by the incarnation of the spirit of God, (in us,) which is going on in us as we grow in holiness. As we grow wise, just, and pure,—in a word, holy,—we grow to be one with him in mode, as we always were in essence. This atonement is effected by *Christ,* only in so far as he taught the manner in which it was to be accomplished more fully than any other, and gave us a better illustration of the method and result in his own person than any one else that has ever lived.

There were, indeed, contradictions, ambiguities, and inconsistencies enough in the new movement to furnish limitless ammunition to any literal-minded critic. There was every variety of speculation, declared Christopher Pearse Cranch, one of the most cosmopolitan though dilettante of the Transcendentalists, but the important thing was "that fresh, earnest, truth-loving and truth-seeking *spirit,* which is abroad." And he added: "As all the mountain tops glow in the coming day, so do all elevated minds feel the coming of a Truth. And without any preconcerted plan—without any inter-communion of minds, the sunlight of Truth seems to flash simultaneously upon lands separated by oceans, by dissimilar languages. On different shores and to insulated minds will the same aspects and applications of truth arise."

Before turning to the crucial question on which Transcendental hopes dashed themselves to their eventual destruction, it is worth noting one other important object of that early expectation: Woman. In part, their attitude was a reflection of the Victorian ideal that put woman on a pedestal, half saint, half simpleton, a rare but breakable ornament. Far from Transcendental circles, in the lusty, materialistic, male society of the frontier, among the ring-tailed roarers who could lick their weight in wildcats, there was a certain awe of the "spirituality" of the female—at least, of the respectable female. (Mark Twain later parodied this bogus spirituality at its most sickly in the figure of Emmeline Grangerford, the frontier "poetess.") There was at the same time, among more sensitive souls in a more developed society, a deeper reaching out to the inward, "feminine" elements of human culture as a counterbalance to the growing domination of crass, extrovert values.

Bronson Alcott all his life anticipated the appearance of a prophetess or "sibyl" who should "speak forth the things of the Spirit as never man had spoken." Neither of the two famous Transcendental women who assisted him for a time in the Temple School—Elizabeth Peabody and Margaret Fuller—qualified for the distinction. Certainly not the ebullient Miss Peabody, who wrote in her diary as a young woman: "I walked along Beacon Street for the first time since we lived in Boston and could but just keep my feet upon the side-walk, so bubble-like and balloony were my sensations. The full, rich foliage, the hills, the water, inflated me. Oh that Common—that Eden in miniature!" Nor could even the overwhelming Miss Fuller, of the richer learning, deeper passions, and more burning energies, be mistaken for the Sibyl that she herself predicted.

In her book *Woman in the Nineteenth Century,* and in an earlier study written for *The Dial,* she set forth her expectations. "No doubt a new manifestation is at hand, a new hour in the day of man." She would have every arbitrary barrier between the sexes thrown down, every path laid open to woman as freely as to man. "Were this done, and a slight temporary fermentation allowed to subside, we believe that the Divine would ascend into nature to a height unknown in the history of past ages." There is but one law for all souls and "if there is to be an interpreter of it, he comes not as man, or son of man, but as Son of God." There is no wholly masculine man, she recognizes, no purely feminine woman:

> It is a vulgar error that love, *a* love to woman is her whole existence; she also is born for Truth and Love in their universal energy. Would she but assume her inheritance, Mary would not be the only Virgin Mother. Not Manzoni alone would celebrate in his wife the virgin mind with the maternal wisdom and conjugal affections. The soul is ever young, ever virgin.
>
> And will not she soon appear? The woman who shall vindicate their birthright for all women; who shall teach them what to claim, and how to use what they obtain? Shall not her name be for her era Victoria, for her country and her life Virginia? Yet predictions are rash; she herself must teach us to give her the fitting name.

The saturnine and skeptical Hawthorne gave a not too flattering portrait of Margaret Fuller in the character of Zenobia in his *Blithedale Romance* (based on the ill-fated Brook Farm experiment). But even he, at the conclusion of *The Scarlet Letter,* sufficiently imbibed the spirit of the age to venture on a prophecy:

> . . . She assured them, too, of her firm belief, that, at some brighter period, when the world should have grown ripe for it, in Heaven's own time, a new truth would be revealed, in order

to establish the whole relation between man and woman on a surer ground of mutual happiness. Earlier in life, Hester had vainly imagined that she herself might be the destined prophetess, but had long since recognized the impossibility that any mission of divine and mysterious truth should be confided to a woman stained with sin, bowed down with shame, or even burdened with a life-long sorrow. The angel and apostle of the coming revelation must be a woman, indeed, but lofty, pure, and beautiful; and wise, moreover, not through dusky grief, but the ethereal medium of joy; and showing how sacred love should make us happy, by the truest test of a life successful to such an end!

Another novelist, the Unitarian clergyman Sylvester Judd, in his *Margaret* exalted woman to the position of leadership in ushering in a new society. One passage between the heroine of this Transcendental-socialistic novel and her future husband records the helplessness of the mere Transcendental dreamer:

[Margaret:] "So you think New Englanders are the best people on the earth?"

[Mr. Evelyn:] "I think they might become such; or rather I think they might lead the august procession of the race to Human Perfectibility; that here might be revealed the Coming of the Day of the Lord wherein the old Heavens of sin and error should be dissolved, and a new Heaven and new Earth be established wherein dwelleth righteousness. I see nothing to prevent our people reassuming the old Hyperionic type, rising head and shoulders to the clouds, crowding out Jupiter and Mars, being filled, as the Apostle says, with all the fulness of God, reaching the stature of perfect man in Christ Jesus, and reimpressing upon the world the lost image of its Maker. . . ."

[Margaret:] "Why don't you lead off yourself in this matter! You shall be a Hero, the days of chivalry shall be renewed."

[Mr. Evelyn:] "I! I have neither health nor spirit. I only perceive, I only deplore."

But when, under Margaret's inspiration, an ideal Christian community has been formed, the erstwhile perceiver-deplorer makes an interesting analysis of woman's capacity for actualizing the ideal:

> Christianity she was unembarrassed to receive, and in that alone has she found a master. . . . I know not that she is a Philosopher, save that she acts philosophically. Our Philosophers, for the most part, by an industrious collation of many facts, like travellers with heavy packs on their shoulders, fare slowly up the hill of their conclusions. On a few facts her conclusions rest; one fact stands with her for many facts, and this from a certain comprehensive and nice power of analogy she possesses. That law by which all facts in the physical, moral and religious world gravitate towards a common centre, and coalesce in one, she has an intuitive perception of. Or rather the soul of all things, the Truth and Love, of which facts are but the signs, she understands by the correspondence of her own soul therewith. Hence is her logic rapid and correct, and her action perfect and sure. She has, perhaps, more Philosophy than a Philosopher. . . .

Even so masculine a figure as Theodore Parker, whose rational, analytical mind scorned the intuitive, synthesizing, "feminine" logic of an Alcott, paid such deference to womanhood as to see it as a necessary element of divinity. The Spirit of Truth would come as a Comforter, Jesus had promised, and for twenty years Parker offered up public prayers each Sunday to "our Father and our Mother God."

Of course, he was not the first to so address the Deity. That early monotheist, Ikhnaton, had declared: "Thou art the mother and the father of all that thou hast made." And the prophet Isaiah had recorded the voice of divinity as saying: "As one whom his mother comforteth, so will I comfort you; and ye shall be comforted in Jerusalem."

Nearer to Boston the Shakers had been saying the same

thing for many years before Parker. Under the leadership of Mother Ann Lee, whom they regarded as the representative of the feminine principle in Deity as Jesus was of the masculine, and as the "Woman clothed with the Sun" described in the Apocalypse, they had come from Old England to New England in 1774, attracted new followers, and established colonies where they mixed celibacy, industry, mysticism, and austere craftsmanship in equal proportions. God they worshiped as Mother as well as Father, and in the official *Life and Gospel Experience of Mother Ann Lee* is found this explanation:

> As *Father,* God is the infinite Fountain of intelligence, and the Source of all power—"the Almighty, great and terrible in majesty"; "the high and lofty one, that inhabiteth eternity, whose name is Holy, dwelling in the high and holy place"; and "a consuming fire." But, as *Mother, "God is Love"* and tenderness. If all the maternal affections of all the female or bearing spirits in animated nature were combined together, and then concentrated in *one individual human female,* that person would be but as a type or image of our Eternal Heavenly *Mother.*
>
> The duality of God is expressed in the *Book of Genesis* as follows: "Let us make man in our image, after our likeness. So God created man in his own image; male and female created He them; and called their name Adam."

This concept seeped through to some of the off-color backwoods prophets: to the Spiritualist–Swedenborgian–Animal Magnetist trance-writer, Andrew Jackson Davis, who wrote of an "intelligent Spiritual Presence . . . the private manifestation of the Father-and-Mother Spirit in each human heart"; to the poet-mystic founder of the Brotherhood of the New Life on the shore of Lake Erie, Thomas Lake Harris, who wrote that "God manifested in the Flesh is not Male merely nor Female merely, but the Two in One," and who also wrote that "God the Wife is the Mother of us all." Less bizarre but more significant is the view of woman held by Phineas Parkhurst Quimby, the mental healer of Portland, Maine, who, starting out as a mesmerist, was groping his way toward a crude idealistic philosophy when the future Mrs. Eddy came to him as a patient. Her impulsive reading of the highest spirituality into his suggestive therapeutics apparently startled but pleased Quimby, who thereafter spoke of himself more than once as a sort of John the Baptist who had need to be taught of the woman who came to him for "pupilage." [4]

This view may be reflected in his comments on the greater spirituality of woman:

> I do not mean that woman means every female. Nor do I pretend to say that man means everything of the animal. But that the mind of the female contains more of that superior substance required to receive the higher development of God's wisdom. For this element is pure love. . . . Then she becomes a teacher of that science which puts man in possession of a wisdom that can subject all animal life to his own control, and separate the wisdom of this world from the wisdom of God. Then woman becomes a teacher of the young, and man stands to woman as a servant to his Lord. . . .

But the obscure miracle-worker of Portland in the early 1860's was a long way from the Boston of thirty years before, where the whole question of miracles had been argued in the highest intellectual circles, with a fervor and a thoroughness seldom equaled elsewhere in history. Here we reach the central religious issue of the times. Of the controversy that raged over miracles one may say what Perry Miller has said of the New England Transcendental hubbub as

---

[4] See Lyman P. Powell, *Mary Baker Eddy: A Life Size Portrait* (New York, Macmillan, 1930), pp. 102, 294. Also Mary Baker Eddy, *The First Church of Christ, Scientist, and Miscellany*, p. 307.

a whole, that "the fascination of this particular tempest, even though it took place in the Boston teacup, is precisely that it churned up prophetic issues." But if it was a tempest, it was also a rock—the rock on which Transcendentalism finally foundered.

3.

Hume in the eighteenth century had proved to the satisfaction of the inductive, empirical mind that there could be no such thing as a miracle. Conservative Boston Unitarians accepted this in general but made an illogical exception of the miracles of Jesus Christ, which they clung to as the only proof of his divinity. The Transcendentalists were both more rational and more mystical in their views. They maintained, as Emerson had beautifully said in *Nature,* that all nature was a miracle and natural law the ever present manifestation of divinity. Thus "special" miracles, such as those attributed to Jesus, were unnecessary. God worked through law, and it was only necessary to clear one's eyes of a befogging materialism in order to see the shining wonder at the heart of each new fact that science brought to light.

But this optimistic acceptance of the universe as experience reveals it was not quite good enough, even for the Transcendentalists. It was all that they got, but they instinctively craved something more. Were there not greater possibilities of control over nature than empirical science offered? Must the miracles of Jesus be surrendered in exchange for the miracles of modern chemistry and geology?

The mild-spirited Channing felt confusedly that the miraculous should *not* be miraculous, and he wrote: "To a man, who cherishes a sense of God, the great difficulty is, not to account for miracles, but to account for their rare occurrence. . . . There is something like coldness and repulsiveness in instructing us only by fixed, inflexible laws of nature.

The intercourse of God with Adam and the patriarchs suits our best conceptions of the relation which he bears to the human race, and ought not to surprise us more, than the expression of a human parent's tenderness and concern towards his offspring."

But that was clearly an old-fashioned view that shied away from the indubitable fact of universal laws of nature. A useful hint, however, could be taken from the German Schleiermacher, who held it inevitable and in accord with a higher law than the understanding (*Verstand*) had yet been able to fathom that Jesus should have been able to perform miracles, which are such only when viewed as isolated phenomena, apart from their connection with his noumenal nature. And the German Hase described the miraculous endowment of Jesus as "a clear dominion of the spirit over nature,—originally conferred upon man at his creation, and regaining its original force through the sinless purity of Jesus, to quell sickness and death; so that there is here no interruption of nature's laws, but only a restoration of her pristine harmony and order."

Similarly, to the question, "But is not a real Miracle simply a violation of the Laws of Nature?" Carlyle had replied: "What are the Laws of Nature? To me perhaps the rising of one from the dead were no violation of these Laws, but were a confirmation; were some far deeper Law, now first penetrated into, and by Spiritual Force, even as the rest have all been, brought to bear on us with its Material Force."

This was the view expounded by Emerson's close friend, William Henry Furness, in his *Remarks on the Four Gospels*, published the same year as *Nature*. Miracles, said Furness, are usually represented as departures from the natural order of things, as interruptions or violations of the laws of nature. But with our present limited knowledge of nature, how can any alleged fact be pronounced a violation of its order? We can observe how things work, but cannot know *why* they thus work or whether they always must; we ascribe events to physical causes but cannot perceive in those physical causes any inherent power to produce the effects by which they are followed. Unless one sees the universe as a soulless machine, what is it that one sees in looking at natural objects and changes? "Nothing, so the reply is commonly expressed, nothing but Mind—nothing but the agency of God. Nothing but the agency of God! In the name of Heaven, what would we have more to stir up the deepest springs of curiosity, wonder and awe, and make us feel that a new world of thought is opened before us!" Everything is seen in a new light. "Natural facts become supernatural, and miracles become natural, when all are regarded as manifestations of an Invisible Mind, an Infinite Will."

This being the case, how can we arbitrarily deny the "miracles" of Jesus? Furness continues:

> I say again, then, that we are not at liberty to pronounce the restoration of a dead man to life, a natural impossibility, or a violation of nature, until we know what death is, and life; what the influence of the mind upon the body, and when the influence ceases, and, more than all, what are the limits of the power with which God may possess a mind of unequalled purity, wisdom and exaltation, like the mind of Jesus Christ, without any violation of the laws of its being.

The question was argued back and forth. To the very un-Transcendental Richard Hildreth, reasoning from a wholly empirical position, nature itself was no miracle or revelation of divinity but simply an object for scientific study, and he wrote:

> Should a person now-a-days, present himself, who had the power, or the apparent power, of restoring the dead to life by a word, or of opening the eyes of the blind merely by com-

manding them to open, howsoever much we might be astonished at these remarkable performances, we should not ascribe them to any supernatural power; we should suppose them to occur in conformity to some law of nature hitherto unknown; and instead of resting in a wondering and superstitious ignorance, the whole science of the age would be turned to discover what that law was.

It was clear that Hildreth himself had no expectation that such a phenomenon would occur; and in this one respect, at least, he agreed with the orthodox Unitarians. The official Unitarian review of Furness' book argued that it was not possible to have a revelation without miracles—miracles that were an actual setting aside of nature's laws—but saw no possibility of new revelations and consequently of new miracles. It rejected with repugnance the view that miracles were simply the manifestation of a higher but universal law:

Mr. Furness's theory represents the miraculous powers of Jesus as native and inherent, as much a part of his intellectual and moral being as the faculties of his understanding, or conscience; and equally liable, in the nature of things, to misapplication, or perversion. . . . But Mr. Furness goes much further than this. We understand him to maintain, that all men are endued with miraculous powers; that the human mind, as such, possesses a "supremacy over" material things. This is to us a very startling proposition; and we do not wonder that he should have anticipated the very obvious objection, that "if it were true, we should have had more numerous manifestations of the wonder-working power of this spiritual law". . . . To us it seems quite incredible, that this mighty energy should have lain dormant and undiscovered, in the human soul from the days of the creation to the time of the Saviour; and still more so, if more could be, that having been once revealed, it should again escape from the consciousness of all men, and require to be discovered anew in the nineteenth century. Here have men been beating their heads for six thousand years against the adamantine bars, within which destiny has encaged them, when all the while they carried, each in his own bosom, a key that might at any moment have set him free. For ourselves, we could as soon believe that a sixth sense remained to be discovered. No *new* power of the human mind, we believe, has been developed since the days of Moses. . . . Mr. Furness intimates, indeed, that glimpses of this consciousness have, from time to time, shown themselves among men, and instances the exorcists in the time of Jesus. The mountebanks of the world, then, as it seems, have been its seers and prophets; and what the profane call quackery is inspiration.

This had the Transcendentalists at a disadvantage. They were able to answer with no miracles of their own. Only on the fringe, among the quacks and mountebanks or the piously naïve and credulous, did that little undercurrent of the "miraculous" continue as it always has through human history. Emerson, in *Nature,* had rounded up such examples as he could, a diversified and indiscriminate list. Complaining that man, in his reliance on ordinary inductive science, applied to nature but half his force, he added:

Meantime, in the thick darkness, there are not wanting gleams of a better light,—occasional examples of the action of man upon nature with his entire force,—with reason as well as understanding. Such examples are, the traditions of miracles in the earliest antiquity of all nations; the history of Jesus Christ; the achievements of a principle, as in religious and political revolutions, and in the abolition of the slave-trade; the miracles of enthusiasm, as those reported of Swedenborg, Hohenlohe, and the Shakers; many obscure and yet contested facts, now arranged under the name of Animal Magnetism; prayer; eloquence; self-healing; and the wisdom of children. These are examples of Reason's momentary grasp of the sceptre, the exertions of a power which exists not in time or space, but an instantaneous instreaming causing power.

But as the years wore on, the bold expectations of a great new influx of spirit, bearing new miracles on its tide, drained away. No "instantaneous instreaming causing power" shaped nature to wonderful, undreamed-of ends; that was left to the new science and the new industrialism, which seemed to bind man more slavishly than ever to the laws of brute nature—even as he learned with dazzling skill to manipulate these laws to his physical advantage. No individual appeared on the scene to vindicate the spirit's effortless lordship over nature; no sudden miracles shook the pillars of established law.

Only Bronson Alcott never gave up hope. "Great Thinker! Great Expecter!" Thoreau apostrophized him, and to the end of his days Alcott retained something of his first Great Expectations. Yet as time went by they seemed more and more to be set within a framework not of effort but of talk. Thoreau had suggested it in the conclusion to his tribute: "Great Thinker! Great Expecter! to converse with whom was a New England Night's Entertainment." There you had it: the miracle was in the conversation, not the deed.

A few years after the failure of the Temple School, Alcott had met with another resounding defeat when he attempted to work the minor miracle of running a Transcendental farm community at "Fruitlands"—where none but the aspiring vegetables were to be eaten and the chief crop turned out to be what his daughter Louisa later described, with rueful affection, as Transcendental wild oats. (Readers of Gandhi's *Autobiography*, however, will realize that the Hindu leader would not have found Alcott's dietary theories funny, and there is enough of a cousinship between Sevagram and Fruitlands to lend a little dignity to the latter's tragicomic failure.) Years afterward Alcott explained that none of them "were prepared to actualize practically the ideal life of which we dreamed," and he commented sadly: "So we fell apart, some returning to the established ways, some soured by the trial, others postponing the fulfilment of his [sic] dream to a more propitious future."

Always the actualizing of Alcott's dream lay ahead in the future. But while the accomplishment tarried, the dreamer talked. The Conversation (capitalized) became his unique mode of expression; in time he came to travel back and forth across the expanding United States holding Conversations (for a modest fee) on philosophical and moral subjects. If society would not allow him to teach its young by this method, then he would kindle in mature minds an awareness of the Divine Idea that would lead to fundamental reforms in education and living. It was as a conversationalist that he had first captured Emerson, though as early as 1842 the latter wrote to Carlyle: "Alcott is a great man, and was made for what is greatest; but I now fear that he has already touched what best he can, and through his more than proph-et's egotism, and the absence of all useful reconciling talents, will bring nothing to pass, and be but a voice in the wilder-ness." And in the same year Emerson wrote in his journal: "It must be conceded that it is speculation which he loves, and not action. . . . When the conversation is ended, all is over. He lives to-morrow as he lived to-day, for further dis-course,—not to begin, as he seemed pledged to do, a new celestial life."

Emerson himself would have been the last one to believe that that conversation, so archangelic and, on occasion, so tedious, had borne *no* fruit. His own experience proved the contrary. "The ideal world," he once wrote, "I might have treated as a cloud-land, had I not known Alcott, who is a native of that country and makes it as solid as Massachusetts for me." To have educated Emerson to a perception of the fundamental reality of the ideal, not as a mere philosophical belief but as a present fact—that might be considered a practical result of some importance. The praise, almost the worship, that Emerson poured at Alcott's feet recurrently through their half-century of friendship is understandable only on these grounds.

There were others, too, whom he influenced deeply. Perhaps the most notable of these was W. T. Harris, who was to become America's leading Hegelian and the first United States Commissioner of Education. Harris thus describes his first meeting with the aging Alcott, on the eve of the Civil War, while he himself was still an undergraduate at Yale:

> It was Mr. Alcott's doctrine of pre-existence, and of the primordial creative power of the soul, which began at once to work a revolution in me. . . . It had not occurred to me that such a thing could be possible. Even if I had read of Berkeley's idealism, or the philosophy of the Neo-Platonists, it had seemed only an eccentricity of thought, rather than a logical necessity of thinking to be studied and comprehended. But here was a living and commanding personality who held a doctrine of the supremacy of the soul and the ideality of the material world. Idealism was not a mere fanciful theory to him, but the sober truth. I concluded that it was worth my time to understand this strange doctrine, which turned topsy-turvy all our current views.

Harris has written a systematic study of Alcott's thought, showing its astonishing subtlety with sufficient particularity to explain to us today why Emerson, as late as 1866, could write of his old friend: "As pure intellect, I have never seen his equal."

But by that time Transcendentalism as a movement was no more than a memory. Parker and Thoreau had burned themselves out and were dead. Margaret Fuller, symbolically enough, had perished in a storm at sea. Others had become disillusioned; one or two, despairing of the "oracle within," had turned to Rome for authority—and perhaps for the "miracles" that Transcendentalism had failed to produce. Emerson's great creative period was past; he would soon be sinking into a gentle old age and gradually losing his memory. Concord was bathed in a golden sunset glow.

Always more worldly wise than his Transcendental fellows, Emerson had seen long before that his initial hopes were too high. "Once we thought positive power was all," he wrote in his essay on Fate. "Now we learn that negative power, or circumstance, is half." All his life the conservative and the radical had balanced precariously in his thought, and both elements remained to the end; but more and more the conservative gained ground, setting limits to what might be expected from the exercise of spiritual power. As a much younger man, he had written: "Men are conservatives when they are least vigorous, or when they are most luxurious. They are conservatives after dinner, or before taking their rest; when they are sick, or aged. In the morning, or when their intellect or their conscience has been aroused; when they hear music, or when they read poetry, they are radicals." And again, writing of the "temper" or temperament with which a man finds himself endowed by fate, he had said: "Men resist the conclusion in the morning, but adopt it as the evening wears on, that temper prevails over everything of time, place and condition, and is inconsumable in the flames of religion. Some modifications the moral sentiment avails to impose, but the individual texture holds its dominion, if not to bias the moral judgments, yet to fix the measure of activity and of enjoyment."

With a very different emphasis Alcott, nearing seventy, wrote in 1868:

> Persist in being yourself, and against fate and yourself. Faith and persistency are life's architects, while doubt and despair bury all under the ruins of any endeavor. You may pull all your paradises about your ears save your earliest; that is to be

yours sometime. Strive and have; still striving till striving is having. We mount to heaven mostly on the ruins of our cherished schemes, finding our failures were successes.

There was little in the world of 1868 to suggest that Transcendentalism's failures were really successes. More and more, during two decades, that early idealism had been gathered into a single channel, the antislavery crusade; and when the Civil War was over and freedom's battle was won, men saw what base and sordid purposes their idealism had led to. The cynical reaction that always follows war set in. A sort of moral exhaustion marked the postwar years. Materialism roared ahead. The wrong people were optimistic for the wrong reasons. Ostentation and bad taste were rampant. The Gilded Age had begun.

Henry Adams, writing of his family's return to the United States in 1868 from England, where his father had been ambassador during the Civil War, declared: "Had they been Tyrian traders of the year B.C. 1000, landing from a galley fresh from Gibraltar, they could hardly have been stranger on the shore of a world so changed from what it had been ten years before." It was the new age of empire building, of dollar worship, of Barnum and Boss Tweed and the robber barons, of lusty revivalism and Irish Catholic immigration, of industrial expansion and industrial strife. What Parrington calls "a passionate will to power" was in evidence; individualism was being "simplified to the acquisitive instinct." Everywhere the ideal seemed to be the "bigger and better," and the bigger was assumed to be necessarily the better.

A surprising number of the new "giants" of the period came from New England, but the energies of the country were pushing westward. Railroads were flung across the continent; even Emerson and Alcott rolled over the prairies on them, taking to distant places a faint echo of the celestial harmonies that had once floated through the woods of Concord.

New England, to be sure, was not all deserted pastures and queer old maids, as its detractors liked to pretend. It was having its Indian summer, which was pleasant enough. Boston could still fancy itself the Hub of the Universe, though its culture grew increasingly genteel and bloodless and unrelated to the vulgar vitality of the age. And there were even signs of a new stirring of the mind there, had any eye been quick enough to catch them.

It was in the early 1870's in Cambridge, across the river from Boston, that a group of thinkers in a loosely formed and loosely named Metaphysical Club discussed the ideas that later took their most characteristic form in the mind of one of them, William James, as pragmatism. Here, in this group of Harvard intellectuals, was the genesis of the philosophy which has usually been considered America's most distinctive contribution to world thought—and which, popularly misunderstood and misapplied, has been taken as the attempted justification of American "materialism." Here was the new form of optimism that was to succeed that of the Transcendentalists: a faith in scientific method, in experiment, in Darwinian "progress," in adaptation to changing environment, in empirical values and concrete results.

James had always admired the utilitarian British emphasis on the "cash value" of an idea, on how the idea *worked*, and it was easy for less scrupulous and less intelligent Americans than he to conclude that any idea was good enough that got quick results. By this popular standard Transcendentalism was a total failure, though James himself found much in Emerson's thinking congenial to his own.

For the 1870's the Darwinian influence was vastly important. It supported the idea of unrestricted competition, of a ruthless struggle for power and survival of the fittest, while at the same time it permitted an ebulliently optimistic interpretation of evolution as progress toward perfection. In this evolutionary optimism, at least, the new Darwinians resembled the old Transcendentalists, but the grounds of their hope were quite different. It was an optimism springing from physical well-being and abundant material opportunity rather than from a faith in the innate divinity of man.

Within this rude optimism lay the seeds of a terrible disillusionment. Even in 1870 they disclosed themselves to one acute young American. Henry Adams had pondered Darwin and his universe of pure chance; but until he saw his sister, hurt in what seemed a trivial accident, die of tetanus after ten days of fiendish agony, he had "never seen Nature—only her surface—the sugar-coating that she shows to youth." It was in Italy where Nature seemed to enjoy the horrible scene, to play with it, to smother her victim with caresses:

> The hot Italian summer brooded outside, over the marketplace and the picturesque peasants; and, in the singular color of the Tuscan atmosphere, the hills and vineyards of the Apennines seemed bursting with midsummer blood. The sick-room itself glowed with the Italian joy of life; friends filled it; no harsh northern lights pierced the soft shadows; even the dying woman shared the sense of the Italian summer; the soft, velvet air, the humor, the courage, the sensual fulness of Nature and man. She faced death, as women mostly do, bravely and even gaily, racked slowly to unconsciousness, but yielding only to violence, as a soldier sabred in battle. For many thousands of years, on these hills and plains, Nature had gone on sabring men and women with the same air of sensual pleasure.

Here was something wholly foreign to American optimism, Transcendental or pragmatic. Nature revealed herself to the stunned Adams as "a nightmare, an insanity of force"; the human mind "felt itself stripped naked, vibrating in a void of shapeless energies, with restless mass, colliding, crushing, wasting, and destroying what these same energies had created and labored from eternity to perfect." The idea "that any personal deity could find pleasure or profit in torturing a poor woman, by accident, with a fiendish cruelty known to man only in perverted and insane temperaments, could not be held for a moment." For pure blasphemy, said Adams, it made atheism a comfort. "God might be, as the Church said, a Substance, but He could not be a Person."

Here the twentieth century already seems to cast its shadow before it. What could the gentle Alcott himself say at such a scene?—unless he could step forth and with the swordlike authority of the Christ whom he desired to emulate banish the nightmare and say to the stricken woman, "Daughter, arise." Even a glimpse ahead into the age of antitetanus serums and sulfa drugs would provide no answer; for the same prophetic glimpse must reveal the multiplied savageries of the coming age—and the writhing schoolgirls at Hiroshima would be small comfort to the sufferer in the Tuscan hills. Could anything less than the demonstrated authority of an irresistible and universal law of good answer the question posed in its starkest form by Adams?

But alas, Alcott could not give that answer, and the rest of America was too busy to think about such things. The shadows were closing in on Concord, though the western sky still glowed. There were still fits and freaks of the old light over the landscape; there were still little expectancies in the air; but the world was rushing by. Down in New York that lonely and almost forgotten giant, Herman Melville—long since back from his desperate encounter with the White Whale of malignity in nature—wrote sardonically:

Found a family, build a state,
The pledged event is still the same:
Matter in end will never abate
His ancient brutal claim.

Walt Whitman, over in Camden, still kept his faith—Whitman, who years ago had been simmering, simmering, simmering until Emerson brought him to the boil, and whom Thoreau and Alcott had journeyed to New York especially to visit—Whitman, lolling in the fields, an old man now but still a kind of perennial boy, never quite grown up, with splendid insights but no answer for Adams—Whitman was writing:

In this broad earth of ours,
Amid the measureless grossness and the slag,
Enclosed and safe within its central heart,
Nestles the seed perfection. . . .

Is it a dream?
Nay but the lack of it the dream,
And failing it life's lore and wealth a dream,
And all the world a dream.

That was fine; but how to prove to a pragmatic age that the solid-seeming ends it sought were really the "dream"? Emerson's old friend, Cyrus Bartol, who had been one of the original members of the Transcendental Club and was now a venerable figure preaching in Boston, wrote wistfully in 1872 of the Transcendentalist of the thirties: "He made consciousness, not sense, the ground of truth; and in the present devotion to physical science, and turn of philosophy to build the universe on foundations of matter, we need to vindicate and reassert his promise." But how? And in the following year, in a book hopefully entitled *The Rising Faith,* he wrote: "Much is said of the coming man. But the woman, his mother, must come before he can! Without a Mary there would have been no Christ. . . . No individual prophet, but a true womanhood is the desire of all nations, redeemer of transgression and Messiah of the world; the heavenly Mother as well as Father we need." [5] The thought is familiar enough, but the words are a little pathetic. The prophetic fire of earlier days is missing. Clearly the time for prophecy was past.

In 1876 Octavius B. Frothingham published his classic account, *Transcendentalism in New England: A History.* The movement was not only dead but embalmed and memorialized. It was forty years since the *annus mirabilis* in which Emerson had published *Nature* and Alcott his *Conversations with Children on the Gospels,* in which the Transcendental Club had been started and Furness had urged that the miracles of Jesus be regarded as "demonstrations of a supreme spiritual force existing in the nature of things." Forty years of wandering in the wilderness—Alcott, Emerson had feared, was destined to be little but a voice in the wilderness—and where was the Promised Land, the promised Comforter, the promised revelation that should make even the desert to blossom as the rose? Was it, indeed, a dream?

---

[5] See also *Absolute Religion* by the Congregationalist Thomas C. Upham, published posthumously in 1873, with its doctrine of Sancta Sophia, or the motherhood within the divine.

CHAPTER TWO

THE FAIR SAINT
AND THE
TEDIOUS ARCHANGEL

[To Mary Baker Eddy:] The sacred truths which you announce, sustained by facts of the Immortal Life, give to your work the seal of inspiration—reaffirm in modern phrase the Christian revelations. In times like ours, so sunk in sensualism, I hail with joy any voice speaking an assured word for God and Immortality. And my joy is heightened the more when I find the blessed words are of woman's divinings.

AMOS BRONSON ALCOTT (1876)

[Of Amos Bronson Alcott:] After the publication of "Science and Health with Key to the Scriptures," his athletic mind, scholarly and serene, was the first to bedew my hope with a drop of humanity. When the press and pulpit cannonaded this book, he introduced himself to the author by saying, "I have come to comfort you." Then eloquently paraphrasing it, and prophesying its prosperity, his conversation with a beauty all its own reassured me. *That prophecy is fulfilled.*

MARY BAKER EDDY (1895)

EARLY IN 1876 Alcott received in the mail a "remarkable volume," as he referred to it in his journal, the gift of a writer unknown to him. The book, which had been published several months earlier, was entitled *Science and Health;* the author was Mary Baker Glover. Always hospitable to new ideas and demanding no prior credentials of a writer, he read it with "profound interest."

Here, for the first time in his life, he found someone with an even greater faith in Spirit than his own. Here, in fact, the whole universe of matter was not merely degraded to the lowest manifestation of Spirit—the outermost rim of the divine manifestation, as the Neoplatonists saw it—but was boldly banished as a baseless misconception of the spiritual

47

universe of God's creating. This differed even from the
Hindu sages who saw the world as *maya*, illusion, but believed that the illusion proceeded as a necessity from the
eternal Brahman or ultimate reality.

The whole point of view of this extraordinary book was,
in fact, far removed from the Upanishadic philosophies with
which Concord was familiar. It did not advocate a contem-
plative withdrawal from the unreal world of sin and sense,
or a mystical absorption in an undifferentiated, all-engulfing
Oneness. It differed even from the more activist Bhagavad-
Gita, the Hindu scripture which appealed most strongly to
the Concord group. It was Christian, meliorative, practical,
with a view of human progress that was as unlike the moral
"detachment" of the Gita as it was unlike the utopian hopes
of the early New England reformers.

It held that human life must be redeemed, not ignored;
that faith must be proved by works; that an acceptance of
Spirit as the very Life of man could begin at once to banish
from experience the grosser forms of illusion, including all
the ills that flesh is heir to. It looked on the healings of Jesus
as natural manifestations of his divine consciousness of reality, and declared that the same Truth he knew and embodied
could produce—and was producing—the same results today
in the healing of physical disease, as well as the reformation
and regeneration of character.

Alcott had had a recurrent, fleeting sense throughout his
life that bodily health should be the inevitable result of
spiritual insight. Almost forty years ago he had written in
his journal, after a bout of toothache: "What a strange and
alien nature is this so-called Pain! The Soul feels him to be
an intruder into her realms, and is restless until she banishes
him thence. Pain gives a man a singular sense of that apparent duality bred by sin, and makes him for the time a be-
liever in its positive being; but when gone into its kingdom

of phantoms, how unreal it is! Pain is Old Sin in a new mask of terms, reappearing to the Soul in the bones and marrow and nerves."

But here was a writer who presented such views not as poetic fancy but as scientific fact, susceptible of pragmatic verification. To be sure, her book was not written in language that the ordinary empirical scientist would regard as scientific; even the idealistic philosopher trained on Plato and Plotinus might find almost insuperable obstacles in it, familiar and acceptable though most of the terms would be to him. There was good, clear, forceful writing to be found in the book, and the style had vitality even when it seemed to lack coherence; but the ideas were hardly developed in the accepted dialectic of philosophical discourse, and the words flowed with an impetuous rush that paid scant attention to literary and even grammatical niceties.[1] Many of the stylistic confusions, as it happened, were due to a careless printer who haphazardly undertook to correct the author's copy without understanding it, and to last-minute restorations, interpolations, and revisions by the author, but others seemed to suggest a thought flooding ahead of the pen, a mind so filled with the urgency of its message that it could not pause for the literary discipline it needed—and which was to come later.

Bronson Alcott, however, could easily make allowance for defects of style in an inspired writer; he was quite willing to accept, with Paul, that "we have this treasure in earthen vessels, that the excellency of the power may be of God,

---

[1] The preface began with a dangling participle: "Leaning on the sustaining Infinite with loving trust, the trials of to-day are brief, and to-morrow is big with blessings." In later editions this became, with a sort of inevitable rightness: "To those leaning on the sustaining infinite, to-day is big with blessings." This change is typical of those which took place in successive revisions of the book, during the course of which it assumed its present title, *Science and Health with Key to the Scriptures.*

and not of us." And he knew the difficulty of expressing ideas that ran contrary to the whole current of accepted thinking. The author herself explained, a little breathlessly, in the preface to her book: "Owing to our explanations constantly vibrating between the same points an irksome repetition of words must occur; also, the use of capital letters, genders and technicalities peculiar to the science, variety of language, or beauty of diction, must give place to close analysis, and unembellished thought." [2]

At any rate, it is clear that Alcott felt in the new book a power that moved him deeply.

The first page sounded not unlike the "prophetic" writings of the Transcendental period:

> ... The wakeful shepherd tending his flocks, beholds from the mountain's top the first faint morning beams ere cometh the risen day. So from Soul's loftier summits shines the pale star to the prophet shepherd, and it traverses night, over to where the young child lies in cradled obscurity that shall waken a world. Over the night of error dawn the morning beams and guiding star of Truth, and the wise men are led by it to Science, to that which repeats the eternal harmony reproduced in proof of immortality and God. The time for thinkers has come; and the time for revolutions, ecclesiastic and social, must come. Truth, independent of doctrines or time-honored systems, stands at the threshold of history. . . . [3]

But as the book moved on, a percipient eye might note that it was separated from the Transcendental writings not only by its more radical attitude toward the material world but by a sort of psychological toughness that was conspicu-

---

[2] Here is a case where the printer may be responsible for the confusion. A period after *science* and a new sentence beginning with *variety* would help to clarify the meaning.

[3] This quotation and those on the next page are from the first edition. Thereafter all quotations from *Science and Health* in this book are from the final, definitive edition unless otherwise designated.

ously lacking from idealists of the utopian breed. "Science lays the axe at the root of error," wrote Mrs. Glover, "and cutting down the belief of Life in matter, of Soul in body, and God in man, exchanges fable for fact, turns thought into new channels away from personality to Principle, through which alone man is able to reach Life." But the denial of corporeal "personality" or the finite, mortal, personal sense of things meant "taking up the cross" in a real and practical sense:

> As progress compels this ripening process through which man resigns the belief of Life and Intelligence in matter, there will be great tribulation such as has not been since the beginning. . . . To suddenly drop our earthly character, and become partakers of eternal Life, without the pangs of a new birth, is morally impossible. We know, "all will be changed in the twinkling of an eye when the last trump shall sound," but the last call of Wisdom is not the first call in the growth of Christian character; while man is selfish, unjust, hypocritical and sensual, to conclude the last call of Wisdom has been heard that awakens him to glorified being is preposterous! Science forbids such feats of imagination, and looks us in the face with reason and revelation.

So much for the perfectionism of an earlier period! Mrs. Glover harbored no illusions about the world's eagerness to accept so self-denying a path to spiritual dominion. She had had "sanguine hopes of its present prosperity," she wrote of her metaphysical system, until she learned "its vastness, the fixedness of folly, and man's hatred of Truth." From then on she was well aware of the "awful conflict" before her.

Alcott, on the other hand, saw no reason for opposition. "Her book," he wrote in his journal for January 17, 1876, "is an earnest and thoughtful appeal to the faith and reason of Christians, and will serve the ends of human culture by its appeals. . . . I cannot vouch for the details of her teachings, but am sure of her having truths to impart deserving the attention of every well-wisher of his race." To the author herself he wrote that often-quoted letter hailing with joy this "assured word for God and Immortality." The perusal of the book, he added, had awakened in him "an earnest desire to know more of yourself personally." He needed "more space than this paper allows to speak discriminatingly of yourself and Science," and concluded: "May I not then enquire if you would deem a visit from me an impertinence? If not, and agreeable to you, will you name the day when I may expect the pleasure of fuller interchange of views on these absorbing themes."

Mrs. Glover most assuredly would not consider a visit from the venerable Mr. Alcott an impertinence, and one was arranged for three days later. Of this visit and of Mrs. Glover herself, Alcott wrote in his journal:

> Leave early with Miss Watson for Boston, and from thence to Lynn, to see Mrs. Glover, who responds to my letter wishing an interview.
>
> She receives me cordially at her house, and I have an interesting visit. I find her one of the fair saints, whose attractions have drawn about her a little circle of followers which meets for fellowship at her house fortnightly, and by whose aid her book has been published. They take the name of "Christian Scientists" and find in the Christian Records the foundation of their faith, the gift of healing as practised by Christ being their central doctrine. Mrs. Glover names hers "Metaphysical Healing"—curing by sympathy with spiritual power over the mind of her patients. Drugs are wholly unused, and her cures have been many.
>
> I find her a devoted student of the New Testament, a Christian in the truest sense, an idealist in apprehending the supremacy of mind over matter, and a faith in Spirit transcending any contemporary whom I have been fortunate to meet.

I shall cultivate further acquaintance with a person of such attractions mentally and spiritually.

As so often with Alcott's descriptions, he is most vague where one could wish him most concrete. What sort of person did he actually find this "fair saint" to be, who possessed such mental and spiritual charms?

Mrs. Glover at that time was a woman of fifty-four, though according to all the available testimony she looked many years younger. There are numerous descriptions of her as she was about this time, from friends and enemies alike, and all paint her as a woman of considerable personal attractiveness, slender, dark-haired, with delicate coloring and those eyes on whose beauty everyone agreed and on whose color everyone differed. "The first thing I noticed about her," wrote a critical young Radcliffe student who visited her a few years later, "was the extraordinary beauty of her eyes—I suppose a novelist would call them violet." [4] Some of her more hostile biographers have tended to slight the deep and favorable impression she made on most people who met her, however violently they might react later; they have also tended to ignore the overwhelming evidence of another characteristic—the warm interest she always showed in the person to whom she was talking.

We may be sure that she felt an intense interest in Bronson Alcott. Here was the first representative of the great world of letters to respond to her book. Her only previous contact with that world had been some years earlier in Amesbury, where she had visited—and healed [5]—Whittier, who himself had written, half metaphorically, half believing in the literal possibility:

---

[4] Mrs. Bernard Berenson in a letter to the author in 1937.
[5] This healing—of a fever and hacking cough—was confirmed to the author a number of years ago by a cousin of Whittier, Mrs. Gertrude Behr (later Barr).

> The healing of His seamless dress
> Is by our beds of pain;
> We touch Him in life's throng and press,
> And we are whole again.

So far Mrs. Glover's followers, since she had held her first class in Lynn in 1870, had been mostly humble shoe workers from the factories of that town—typically New England products, men and women with inquiring minds and simple faith, but with horizons somewhat bounded by the little world they moved in. Alcott must have been to Mrs. Glover a breath of exhilarating air from a larger intellectual sphere, as she was to him a revelation of deeper reliance on spiritual power than he had before encountered.

As to her mental or intellectual attractions, to which he referred, it is clear that Mrs. Glover was neither the paragon of academic scholarship which some have imagined her to be nor the backwoods Emmeline Grangerford that others have painted her as being. Her education had been irregular because of ill health, but included coaching by a brother who was an outstandingly brilliant student at Dartmouth, with a strong bent toward metaphysics. Her searching mind obviously led her to read widely—or at least deeply—among such books and periodicals as were available to her in the communities where she lived. Her scattered early writings ranged from period pieces for *Godey's Lady's Book* to the following meditation on the Immortality of the Soul, published in *The Covenant*, organ of the International Order of Odd Fellows, in 1847 when she was a young widow of twenty-six:

> . . . Who does not sometimes conjecture what will be his condition and employment in eternity? Will the mind be continually augmenting its stock of knowledge, and advancing toward complete perfection? It cannot be otherwise.

We shall there apprehend fully the relations and dependencies incomprehensible to understandings encircled by clay. The boundless ocean of truth will be fathomed and investigated by those, whom, like Newton, a residence here scarcely acquainted with a few pebbles on its trackless shore. The result of all experiments will then be satisfactory, since they will accord with the deductions of enlarged and enlightened reason.

Most authors have but dimly shadowed forth their own imaginings, and much of what they intended is involved in obscurity. This makes an approach to the regions of science and literature so extremely difficult; there this obstacle will be removed. No veil will hide from our observation the beauties, lovely, inimitable, of wisdom and philosophy; all their charms will there be displayed.

The imperfection of language will be no hindrance to the acquisition of ideas, as it will no longer be necessary as a me dium of thought and communication. Intelligence, refined, etherealized, will converse directly with material objects, *if indeed, matter be existent. . . .*[6]

Besides the evident influence of eighteenth-century models on her writing, this piece is interesting chiefly for the last phrase quoted, which suggests the direction her thought was already taking. There is no evidence that its radical idealism was particularly shaped by contemporary philosophic influences, for through two crucial decades of increasing invalidism and financial stringency, she was largely isolated from new books and intellectual currents in the remote towns and villages where she lived. Her scrapbooks of the period indicate that the Transcendental ferment almost totally escaped her.

---

[6] Vol. 6, No. 5 (May, 1847), pp. 193–94. Italics added. In a girlhood poem, written some years before, occurred the lines:

But hope, as the eaglet that spurneth the sod,
May soar above matter, to fasten on God.

(Quoted in her autobiography, *Retrospection and Introspection,* p. 18.)

Instead, she had turned wholeheartedly to the Bible for inspiration, and concurrently to the new school of homeopathy for healing. Experiments in the latter and her subsequent experience with Quimbyism intensified her conviction that all disease was mental and that the true principle of healing was that which lay behind Jesus' cures. In 1866, after Quimby's death, she herself had a striking healing which she came to recognize as the decisive moment of "revelation" in her own development. "That brief experience," she wrote later, "included a glimpse of the great fact that I have since tried to make plain to others, namely, Life in and of Spirit; this Life being the sole reality of existence. . . . That there is but one God or Life, one cause and one effect, is the *multum in parvo* of Christian Science; and to my understanding it is the heart of Christianity."

Of themselves, these words might almost have been written by any of the Transcendentalists. But there is a great difference. When she said "sole reality" she meant sole reality. To her that fact was as all-engulfing a revelation as any that Paul received on the road to Damascus. And if true, it must be demonstrated. It took her almost ten years of "hard work," she said, before she was ready to publish her textbook in 1875, for she had learned "that this Science must be demonstrated by healing, before a work on the subject could be profitably studied." She would have agreed with Emerson: "Metaphysics is dangerous as a single pursuit. . . . It must be perpetually reinforced by life, must be the observations of a working man on working men, must be biography—the record of some law whose working was surprised by the observer in natural action."

Alcott found her, he said, "a devoted student of the New Testament," and any interpretation of her that misses this point misses the essence of her character. For her thought was rooted in the Bible, and particularly the New Testament;

her language was drawn from it; she turned to it naturally and constantly for inspiration, instruction, and illustration.

Take the matter of pre-existence. Possibly she and Alcott were the only two people of any stature in New England who believed in the pre-existence of the soul. It was not an orthodox Christian doctrine, and Alcott had taken it largely from Plato and Plotinus; but Mrs. Glover drew it directly from the Bible as she understood it. When Jesus declared, "Before Abraham was, I am," he was speaking, she held, of his divine selfhood, the Christ, the eternal manifestation of the one, ever-present I Am. But the Christ embraced the true identity of all men, existing outside matter in a timeless realm of perfect, spiritual being. Behind the mistaken, finite, temporal concept of being which formed the corporeal person—and shining through it in varying measure—was the pre-existent spiritual identity, the faultless Son of God, the Christ-idea with healing in its wings.

How much of this the two may have touched on in their visit together we do not know. A few days later Alcott wrote in his journal with a slight note of apology: "To Boston for deafness and dentistry. One may not be ashamed of needing a little mending at the age of seventy-six." Forty years earlier Emerson, writing of man's reliance on the lower "understanding instead of the reason," had said: "His relation to nature, his power over it, is through the understanding, as by manure; the economic use of fire, wind, water, and the mariner's needle; steam, coal, chemical agriculture; the repairs of the human body by the dentist and the surgeon. This is such a resumption of power as if a banished king should buy his territories inch by inch, instead of vaulting at once into his throne." But at seventy-six Alcott had no expectation of vaulting at once into his throne, even with Mrs. Glover's help. He had seen too many promises fail, too many wonders fade, not to have learned to accommodate himself to the world as he must live in it. Utopian though he remained, he found it wiser to postpone Utopia to the day after tomorrow.

An interesting hint of this caution occurs in his next letter to Mrs. Glover, written a few days later. It is worth quoting in its entirety:

> Concord January
> 30th 1876.

DEAR MRS. GLOVER,

My visit left pleasant memories and opens agreeable prospects.

Faith Hope and Charity, are graces so rare in our modern life, that one comes within their presence with something akin to wonder and sweet surprise. I certainly shall wish to meet with your devoted circle only let me know when and how I may be permitted that privilege. I wish to learn and have not undocile ears.

Last Sunday evening I met a pleasant circle at Mr Emersons, and took occasion to speak of yourself, your Science and disciples. Mr Emerson had heard of your book, it appeared, and the company listened to what I had to tell without disloyal criticism.

In such ways, I shall best advertise your self and your Science.

Next Wednesday evening, I am to meet the Divinity Students at Cambridge for Conversation on Divine Ideas and methods. I think you may safely trust my commendations of your faith and methods anywhere.

Hoping to meet you again for more intimate fellowship,

> I am, Cordially Yours,
> A. BRONSON ALCOTT

Mrs. M. B. Glover

The company at Emerson's had listened to his account of Mrs. Glover and her Science "without disloyal criticism." Here is the telltale phrase. One can almost feel the slight chill in the air as Alcott brought up his latest enthusiasm at the Sunday-evening gathering. These chastened Transcendentalists had long since ceased to believe in miracles or to look for new revelations. Only Alcott remained incorrigibly expectant—incorrigibly gullible, in their eyes. Still they were loyal to their valued old friend (there could hardly be any question of loyalty to the unknown Mrs. Glover) and would listen politely and ask a few questions and murmur, "How interesting."

Yet Alcott's phrase showed that he felt the chill, and that it checked a little the course of his own enthusiasm. "Great Expecter!" Thoreau had called him; but he had not lived seventy-six years and encountered repeated failure of his most cherished schemes for actualizing the ideal without learning to distrust a little his own radical sense of what was possible in human life. The reaction of Emerson's circle to his talk about Mrs. Glover's "Science" was a reminder not to forget "the restraining grace of common sense," as Emerson called it. And so, even while he wrote to her with some eagerness and noted in his journal that he would gladly meet her disciples and "learn what they have for me, with docile ears and heart," he added a cautionary note. In the same journal entry he repeated, with a slight variant, his remark about coming within the presence of Faith, Hope, and Charity "with something of wonder and sweet surprise," but added: "Even if disappointed at finding one's wonder and surprise too adventurous for their novelty, his experience may be serviceable nevertheless. 'Believing all things' is scriptural, at least." The Sunday evening had sown its seed of doubt.

A week later he wrote Mrs. Glover again. The letter explains itself:

> On returning from Cambridge, I find your kind note.
> It would give me pleasure to meet your Class of Initiation tomorrow, but I must content myself with the hope of attend-

ing your monthly service—of which I shall wish to be informed in due time, both as to the day and hour of meeting.

I have had occasion to commend yourself and book to respectful consideration, more than once, and to some of our best people. I judge your worst opponents will be found among professing saints, and worthless men.

I trust you will be able to show that devils of all professions are cast out by prayer and fastings.

The invitation had evidently come with unexpected suddenness; hence the wish to be informed "in due time" of any further meetings. In the leadership of her movement, the founder of Christian Science frequently had occasion to summon people to her side rather suddenly. There was a tremendous work to be done, vast obstacles to be dissolved into their "native nothingness," fierce opposition to overcome by demonstrating the omnipotence of the divine Principle, Love. Could not even the renowned Mr. Alcott feel the urgency of the challenge? Mr. Alcott, who looked forward merely to "the pleasure of fuller interchange of views on these absorbing themes," could not. And while he knew the force of opposition and the sting of public contempt and could sympathize with Mrs. Glover's difficulties, his present serenity must have seemed to him a proof of what a little "prayer and fasting" could do.

Besides, the people to whom he spoke about Mrs. Glover's Science did not seem to be violently opposed to it—a bit cool, perhaps, but not hostile. The attitude of "some of our best people" may perhaps be typified by Longfellow's urbane acknowledgment to Mrs. Glover of a copy of her book: "Having so many occupations and interruptions, I have not found time to read 'Science and Health' sufficiently, but will not on that account delay thanking you for its excellence."

The next day one of Mrs. Glover's students, George Barry,

came out to Concord. Alcott had met this simple, freshfaced young man on his earlier visit to Lynn and had been much taken with him. When he had asked Barry his age, the young man had replied promptly, "Five years old, sir"—explaining that it was five years since he had first studied with Mrs. Glover. That was the effect her teachings seemed to have on her students: they felt "reborn" into a wonderful new world of Spirit. Barry had been healed of consumption by Mrs. Glover; his devotion to her knew no bounds; and he served her in every way possible. He was the first of her students to ask if he might call her "Mother," and had written a poem to her which ran:

> O, mother mine, God grant I ne'er forget,
> Whatever be my grief or what my joy,
> The unmeasured, unextinguishable debt
> I owe to thee, but find my sweet employ
> Ever through thy remaining days to be
> To thee as faithful as thou wast to me.

In view of his later development, the lines take on a sadly ironic flavor.

Alcott's entry in his journal indicates that young Barry made a good impression but struck him as pretty naïve by the intellectual standards of Concord:

Mr. Barry, a disciple of Mrs. Glover, dines, and gives us information concerning Mrs. G's practice in healing. An interesting young gentleman, bearing favorable testimony to the faith and purity of the school.

I give him copies of "The Philosophemes," with a number or two of *The Journal of Speculative Philosophy*. A wider acquaintance with idealism in its various phases will be serviceable to these "Metaphysical Healers" and "Christian Scientists," as they call their school.

Another journal entry four days later has a similar tone.

Something has taken the bloom off Alcott's enthusiasm in the three weeks since his delighted visit to Lynn:

Mrs. Glover writes inviting me to meet the "Christian Scientists" at her house on Wednesday evening next, for consultation and discussion. I am interested in this professed metaphysical science, and shall listen curiously to what may be shown or suggested on that occasion. A hospitable eye and open ear best befit the scholar and thinker, especially as regards any fresh insight into humanity.

In answering Mrs. Glover's note, he referred kindly to Barry's visit: "Mr. Barry made us a pleasant visit and interested us by his modesty and intelligence." He would endeavor to meet her friends, the Christian Scientists, at her house next Wednesday evening: "You very kindly propose my remaining over night in Lynn. This will give me full time to continue till the close of your session." Mrs. Alcott would unfortunately be unable to accompany him, as she seldom left home and then only for a short ride about the village. Mr. Sanborn of the Springfield *Republican* had Mrs. Glover's book "and should find much to respect in its spirit and teachings." He had not written "the worthless notice which you sent me."

The journal entry for the next Wednesday, February 16, reads:

5 P.M. Leave for Lynn. Dr. Spofford takes me to The Falkland House, where I take tea, and meet, afterwards, Mrs. Glover's circle at her house in Broad Street. The evening is passed in discussing metaphysical problems. I find her followers thoughtful and devout, without cant or egotism, students of life rather than of books, and a promising company. The slight touch of mysticism mingling with their faith renders them the more interesting, and Mrs. Glover's influence appears to be of the happiest character. Our conversation continues till near 11 o'clock. I sleep at the Falkland House.

she did write to Alcott about both these things within the next fortnight is indicated by his letter of March 5 to her:

> I can assure you that I learned nothing but praise of yourself and followers during my visit at Lynn. Nor have I elsewhere before that or since. And you must have felt that I was more than pleased with your circle and yourself on that evening at your room.
>
> If I can serve you at this time, please inform me either by letter or in a personal interview.
>
> I shall be in Boston some day this week, having a *"Conversation"* at Somerville. I have not yet learned on what evening definitely.
>
> If most convenient and proper I might ride out and see you at Lynn.
>
> Truth, you know, has to run the gauntlett on all sides to triumph over adversaries, and honor itself.

It did not turn out to be "convenient and proper" for Alcott to make the visit. But Mrs. Glover evidently took seriously his offer to "serve" her; for Spofford, who was handling the publicity for *Science and Health,* wrote him a day or two later asking permission to use in an advertisement a quotation from his first letter to her in praise of the book. Alcott replied:

> I shall be quite willing Mrs. Glover should use any part of my letter in Commendation of her book in any manner which she may think likely to bring its theories and methods to the notice of readers.
>
> A method so contrary to received opinions, and a faith so spiritual as hers, must of necessity encounter popular prejudice, and its truths proved by unquestioned facts, and many such. Meanwhile, Mrs. Glover, I am persuaded will maintain the spirit and manners of a true disciple of the views which commend themselves to her faith and practice.

The last sentence is revealing. Mrs. Glover lived for one purpose only: to bring her revelation of reality to a world sunk in materialism. In the last analysis nothing else mattered. When Alcott talked with her and her small "circle" he was deeply impressed by the spiritual force of their faith and its fruits. But once away from them he felt the chilling skepticism of a world that had long ago chastened his own highest expectations. His great days of battle were over; he had come to terms with an order of things which permitted his kind of idealism as a conversational luxury but which could hardly be expected to tolerate so direct a challenge to its legitimacy as Mrs. Glover offered. Despite his kindly desire to help, he may have felt that she was pushing a little beyond the bounds of propriety in making her request.[9] It was up to her, after all, to see that the unpopular truths she taught were "proved by unquestioned facts, and many such."

No one was more aware of this necessity than Mrs. Glover, who was laboring night and day to cultivate in her students the spiritual understanding that would bring forth increasing "demonstrations" of Christian power. In the midst of this exacting task she could hardly let her sense of the appropriate be governed by Alcott's delicate sensibilities.

There was one more interchange a few days later, when he wrote her:

Thanks for your book forwarded by express.

I have given a copy to Mr. Sanborn, and one to Mrs. Johnson, whom I met a year since at the West, and who was here yesterday. She appears to entertain views much in harmony with yours as regards healing and Christian influences. I com-

---

[9] Twenty years earlier, Emerson had written a letter to the author of *Leaves of Grass*, hailing him "at the beginning of a great career," and expressing a wish to meet him. But when the winds of controversy blew about that remarkable book, Emerson complained to a friend that Whitman "had done a strange rude thing in printing in the *Tribune* . . . my letter of thanks for his book." Whitman, it appears, had not even asked permission.

mended her to Dr. Spofford, hoping that you would favor her with an interview.

The other copy of your book I reserve for our "Concord Library."

After that, the correspondence lapsed for a year.

2.

A period of storm and stress was opening for the little band of Christian Scientists. Mrs. Glover was fighting for the life of her movement. Everything must be subordinated to this single end. Action was very definitely a part of the Christian Science program; and action of the sort that Mrs. Glover demanded, Alcott was obviously unable and unwilling to give. "Love," she admonished her followers energetically, "is not something put upon a shelf, to be taken down on rare occasions with sugar-tongs and laid on a rose leaf. I make strong demands on love, call for active witnesses to prove it, and noble sacrifices and grand achievements as its results."

Grateful as she was for Alcott's friendship, she was unable to give herself up to the sweets of conversation, as he would have desired (though in later years she recalled how "his conversation with a beauty all its own reassured me"). She was, in a sense, working in the grime of human life in a way that Alcott was never willing to do, coming to grips with the passions, prejudices, and cross-purposes of the ordinary people around her in an effort to heal and awaken them. Christian Science as she conceived it was no transcendental philosophy for the occasional visionary or speculative thinker; it must *work* in the very face of small minds, petty personal spites, deep-lying resistance, and malice.

Yes, malice. For the counterpoise to Mrs. Glover's vision of the divine Mind and its creation as wholly spiritual and

wholly good was her gradual conviction of the total ignorance and malice of what she called "mortal mind"—the false
supposition of a life apart from God. Paul had truly said,
"The carnal mind is enmity against God." And Jesus himself,
the infinitely compassionate, had addressed with harsh
words the material mentalities which conspired to murder
him: "Ye are of your father the devil, and the lusts of your
father ye will do. He was a murderer from the beginning,
and abode not in the truth, because there is no truth in him.
When he speaketh a lie, he speaketh of his own: for he is a
liar, and the father of it."

That passage of Scripture was not popular with the liberal
Christians of the nineteenth century, who had thrown out
hell-fire as obviously unworthy of a loving God, and hoped
thereby to have exorcised hell from the dark depths of human nature—if, indeed, they recognized that it had ever been
there. Was not man obviously and naturally good, and was
not human advancement inevitable? The torture chambers
and gas ovens of Dachau and Buchenwald were a long way
off; the mushrooming violence of scientific "progress" was
as yet unthinkable. Emerson had written: "There is no pure
lie, no pure malignity in nature. The entertainment of the
proposition of depravity is the last profligacy and profana-
tion. There is no scepticism, no atheism but that. Could it
be received into common belief, suicide would unpeople the
planet."

If he had said that there was no pure lie or malignity in
God or God's creation, Mrs. Glover would have agreed. She
had rebelled even in childhood against a Calvinism which
essentially taught that. But she retained something of the
Calvinistic iron that enabled her to confront without flinch-
ing the element of sheer lie, sheer ignorance, sheer malice in
nature, as experienced and represented by the "natural man."
Far better than Emerson she would have understood what

Henry Adams meant when he saw nature as an insanity of force casually murdering its helpless victims. Surely that was the nature of mortal mind, of the atheistic supposition that man could be mortal, could be separate from the divine Life, could be a prisoner of the matter-stuff of mortal mind's own perverted conceiving.

Mrs. Glover was well aware that the "dream of mortal existence" could at any moment become a nightmare. She did not expect the dream to become more and more pleasant. She expected the dreamer more and more to awake—to claim his pre-existent selfhood in God, intact and perfect, and thereby to see the dream gradually fade away, both in its hideous and its seductive phases. She drew a sharp distinction between the earthly and the divine. "Mortals are not the children of God," she wrote. "Far from it."

All that was good, wise, loving, and lovely she saw as a manifestation of the divine Mind, but all that would limit, oppose, pervert, and destroy this manifestation she saw as a false concept of the carnal mind. Thus the task of the awakened consciousness was to manifest the man of God's creating, but this required the dropping of all illusions about what, with supreme realism, she called "the ghastly farce of material existence." Of the person content to dream along in materialism she wrote: "I can conceive of little short of the old orthodox hell to waken such a one from his deluded sense." Some mortals, she went on with ironic exaggeration, "may even need to hear the following thunderbolt of Jonathan Edwards," and she quoted from the notorious Enfield sermon:

> It is nothing but God's mere pleasure that keeps you from being this moment swallowed up in everlasting destruction. He is of purer eyes than to bear to have you in His sight. There is no other reason to be given why you have not gone to hell since you have sat here in the house of God, provoking His

pure eyes by your sinful, wicked manner of attending His solemn worship. Yea, there is nothing else that is to be given as a reason why you do not at this moment drop down into hell, but that God's hand has held you up.

And again her language is reminiscent of Calvinism when she announces:

The signs of these times portend a long and strong determination of mankind to cleave to the world, the flesh, and evil, causing great obscuration of Spirit. When we remember that God is just, and admit the total depravity of mortals, *alias* mortal mind,—and that this Adam legacy must first be seen, and then must be subdued and recompensed by justice, the eternal attribute of Truth,—the outlook demands labor, and the laborers seem few.

This is not the central emphasis of her teaching, but it runs through as a recurrent theme and is an essential part of it— not an irrelevant contradiction, as superficial critics have maintained. It would be totally foreign to Transcendentalism, but Christian Science is not Transcendentalism: it does not represent (as Christian Scientists see it) the human mind claiming to be God or the emanation of God, but it discloses the human mind as retiring before the divine Mind, as "giving up the ghost" or any pretension to be an entity in itself. Christian Science says, in the words that lie at the heart of Christianity, "Not my will, but Thine, be done." But it sees them as words of hope, not of resignation, as the gateway to the demonstration, here and now, in increasing measure, of the Life that is God.

Mrs. Glover was later to write that while the truth of God's allness and goodness had flowed into her thought as naturally as the morning light spills over the horizon, she shrank from investigating the dark lie about God and man which constitutes the illusion of mortal existence.

The first great shock had come to her in 1872 when one of her earliest students had decided that what he was practicing was nothing but "mesmerism," and another student gave practical evidence that Christian Science to him was nothing but mental suggestion. That anyone could so totally misunderstand her teachings seemed almost incredible; here was a sharp indication of the difficulty many mentalities were to have in grasping even the rudiments of divine healing. To her, "mesmerism" was identical with anti-Christ. She saw the hypnotic control of one human mind over another as the very antithesis of Christian Science practice, in which the human mind must yield to the divine. To dispossess a person of his God-given individuality seemed to her the ultimate horror. Eventually she came to see all error as hypnotic in nature, inducing belief in that which had no substantive existence in the divine Mind. Mortal mind was the basic "mesmerist," acting through what she called "aggressive mental suggestion."

The techniques of modern advertising, with their insistent appeals to the vanity, cupidity, fear, and appetite of the unwary, had not then been developed. Modern dictatorship had not then appeared with its psychological arsenal of repetitive propaganda, the big lie, control of mass media, political commissars, brainwashing, thought control, to illustrate the potentialities of aggressive mental suggestion on the grand scale. Modern psychology had not then explored the phenomena of hysteria and hypnosis and that whole dark world of the unconscious about which it still knows so little.[10]

---

[10] Cf. Freud: "No doubt you would prefer that I hold fast to a moderate theism, and turn relentlessly against anything occult. But I am not concerned to seek anyone's favor, and I must suggest to you that you should think more kindly of the objective possibility of thought-transference and therefore also of telepathy." (*New Introductory Lectures in Psycho-Analysis*)

Cf. also Jung's comment on the "old religions" with their "horrible symbols": "At any time they may break in upon us with destructive force,

But Mrs. Glover was already teaching that man's sole defense against the antirational, disintegrative force of the human will acting through conscious or unconscious suggestion is an understanding of and yielding to the divine will, which at all times is saying, "Let there be light."

She borrowed from the vocabulary of her times a useful term to describe this illusory force opposing itself to the light-bringing Christ. She called it "animal magnetism," and the phrase has suggestiveness in the context of today's biology and physics. But it also retains some of its original suggestion of an occult influence operating at some subrational level of consciousness. Years before Freud, Mrs. Glover was writing about the "unconscious" stratum of mortal mind in which sin or disease might originate. In a sermon delivered in Boston ten years later she was to declare, speaking of the popular spiritualism:

> When I learned how mind produces disease on the body, I learned how it produces the manifestations ignorantly imputed to spirits. I saw how the mind's ideals were evolved and made tangible; and it matters not if that ideal is a flower or a cancer, if the belief is strong enough to manifest it. . . . The belief that produces this result may be wholly unknown to the individual, because it is lying back in the unconscious thought, a latent cause producing the effect we see.

According to Christian Science, the remedy for all such unconscious error is the conscious identification of oneself with the infinite light of intelligence pouring forth from the divine Mind. But "personal sense," Mrs. Glover discovered, argued against such an identification—argued for its own opinions and predilections and for the domination of its own will. The animal instinct in mortals caused them to cry out,

in the form of mass-suggestion, for example, against which the individual is defenceless. Our frightful Gods have only changed their names." (*Two Essays on Analytical Psychology*) like the "unclean spirit" in the man healed by Jesus: "Let us alone; what have we to do with thee, thou Jesus of Nazareth? art thou come to destroy us? I know thee who thou art, the Holy One of God." Or to claim, with the more sophisticated malice of those who consciously plotted to murder Jesus: "This fellow doth not cast out devils, but by Beelzebub the prince of the devils"—this so-called Christ-healing is nothing but the hypnotic control of one mind by another.

This, as Mrs. Glover saw it, was the background of the period of turbulence that opened in 1876. The coming of a new student, Asa Gilbert Eddy, into the little circle seemed to precipitate it. This quiet, mild-mannered man soon became a successful practitioner, and Mrs. Glover came to rely more and more on his faithful devotion and willingness to serve the cause at whatever cost to himself. It has been suggested that jealousy of the newcomer's position in the group accounts for the sudden and violent change that took place in young George Barry's attitude toward his teacher about this time. It would seem to be the occasion for that change, but the cause probably lies deeper—as deep, according to Mrs. Glover's teaching, as the inherent malice of the carnal mind toward the demands of Spirit. Barry's defection was but one of many cases where students of hers who had looked up to her as a saint, a loving guide and friend, came to regard her, in a dramatic revulsion of feeling, as a tyrant and a fraud.

Unfriendly biographers have put their own interpretation on the phenomenon. Obviously, they say, these bedazzled students had simply freed themselves from the "magnetism" of her personality and looked the "facts" in the face—like the little defecting group that several years later accused her of "frequent ebullitions of temper, love of money, and the appearance of hypocrisy." But such an interpretation fails to account for an enormous amount of evidence to the contrary, for indubitable facts which stubbornly refuse to fit into this kind of explanation. The easiest path for these biographers has been simply to omit the facts that embarrass their theories. An honorable exception has been the British historian, H. A. L. Fisher, in his book *Our New Religion* (London and New York, Jonathan Cape, 1930). Though he writes excoriatingly of Christian Science and its founder, his intellectual honesty compels him to make such admissions as these, which sit very oddly in the midst of his repellent picture of her in the terms made familiar and fashionable by a long line of critics: "Prayer, meditation, eager and puzzled interrogation of the Bible, had claimed from childhood much of her energy, so that those who met her in later times were conscious of a certain quiet exaltation, such as may come to a woman nursing a secret spiritual advantage. . . . Upon many of her intimates she made the impression of a saint. The great ideas of God, of immortality, of the soul, of a life penetrated by Christianity, were never far from her mind."

Here one is getting closer to the heart of the matter. The discoverer of Christian Science is understandable only in terms of that which she discovered—of that which became the very substance of her thinking, her prayers, her striving. "Christian Science," she declared some years later, "is my only ideal; and the individual and his ideal can never be severed." Since the heart and soul of Christian Science is avowedly love, it is hardly surprising that the testimony of hundreds of people who knew her during the last forty years of her life should bear witness to one outstanding quality— a deep, self-sacrificing, compassionate Christian love. Years after her death many of those who knew her best (and some of whom I came to know while a student at Harvard) could hardly speak of her without tears filling their eyes, even while their faces lighted up with an affection more revealing than anything they could say.

Yet these people, to my observation, were not flabby sentimentalists; they were men and women of considerable strength of character, intelligence, and experience. Nor was their Leader a sentimentalist, for all the little Victorian touches that sometimes decorated her style. Love, as she understood it, was not a sentiment but a Principle—a Principle that could be inexorable on the dishonest, the self-indulgent, the self-willed, the proud. It is one of the profound paradoxes of the religious life—exemplified once and for all in the crucifixion of the Prince of Peace—that the divinest love should be felt by the world as a kind of intolerable discomfort, bringing not peace but a sword. "If they have called the master of the house Beelzebub, how much more shall they call them of his household?" "Woe unto you, when all men shall speak well of you!" "They hated me without a cause."

Perhaps nowhere in modern literature is this hard paradox more penetratingly explored than in the chapter in *Science and Health* on "Atonement and Eucharist," into which, as it developed through successive editions, the author poured her heart's deepest experience. Elsewhere she quotes the report supposed to have been made by a contemporary of Jesus: "His rebuke is fearful," and points for illustration to his own stern words to Peter: "Get thee behind me, Satan." Yet the rebuke, she makes clear, was to "error," not to person; and it was thus she viewed the disciplinary aspect of her own leadership, when, like the surgeon, she must wound to heal. To many of her early followers, however—small people, kindled by her vision but unable to keep pace with the extraordinary growth of her thought—it seemed impossible to rise above their limited personal sense to the magnitude of the task to which she called them, and to such there would come a day when what had been all light became all darkness.

Certainly Mrs. Glover made "strong demands" on her followers, as she herself said; but she made even stronger demands on herself.[11] Moreover, she was exploring an uncharted mental ocean where, as she wrote, "incredible good and evil elements" were coming to the surface. She was touching raw nerves; she was putting a tremendous strain on ordinary human nature. Through experience she had to learn how much her students could stand.

In her very first class in 1870 there had been a young seaman who had joined it after his brother was healed of tuberculosis, but without giving any particular thought to what he expected to learn. When, as a result of his first lessons, he cured a girl of dropsy, he was so startled that he dropped the new teaching like a hot potato. Others, to whom the same teaching seemed to alter the whole face of the earth, tearing away the veil of matter to reveal a world of wholly mental forces, found themselves facing starker challenges than they had anticipated. The measure of the greatness of a new idea may be the dislocation of human thought it causes. We recognize, in the physical world, that the introduction of the atomic bomb into the world is bound to cause convulsive political reactions and dangerous psychological tensions; but the spiritual energy that Mrs. Glover's teaching released in that little world of Lynn was as far in advance of the usual forms of Christian influence known to it as atomic power is in advance of hitherto available forms of physical energy.

---

[11] One of her students found her a year or two later scrubbing the back stairs because she was unable to get any help; and when he uttered a shocked protest, she replied cheerfully that "it was good for her after sitting at her writing table for so many hours." (Reminiscences of Arthur True Buswell, quoted in *The Genealogy and Life of Asa Gilbert Eddy*, by Mary Beecher Longyear, Brookline, Mass., privately printed, 1922.)

A single instance will illustrate this in a measure. Mrs. Miranda Rice, who wrote the following account, and her sister, Dorcas Rawson, later turned against Mrs. Glover (then Mrs. Eddy) with intense bitterness; but though they furnished hostile journalists with all sorts of ammunition against their former teacher, they could not be shaken in their insistence that this incident occurred exactly as related:

I take pleasure in giving to the public one instance, out of the many, of Mrs. Glover-Eddy's skill in metaphysical healing. At the birth of my youngest child, now eight years old, I thought my approaching confinement would be premature by several weeks, and sent her a message to that effect. Without seeing me, she returned answer that the proper time had come, and that she would be with me immediately. Slight labor-pains had commenced before she arrived. She stopped them at once, and requested me to call an accoucheur, but to keep him below stairs until after the birth. When the doctor arrived, and while he remained in a lower room, Mrs. Eddy came to my bedside. I asked her how I should lie. She answered, "It makes no difference how you lie," and added, "Now let the child be born." Immediately the birth took place, and without a pain. The doctor was then called into the room to receive the child, and he saw that I had no pain whatever. My sister, Dorcas B. Rawson, of Lynn, was present when my babe was born, and will testify to the facts as I have stated them. I confess my own astonishment. I did not expect so much, even from Mrs. Eddy, especially as I had suffered before very severely in childbirth. The physician covered me with extra bedclothes, charged me to be very careful about taking cold and to keep quiet, and then went away. I think he was alarmed at my having no labor-pains, but before he went out I had an ague coming on. When the door closed behind him, Mrs. Eddy threw off the extra coverings and said, "It is nothing but the fear produced by the doctor that causes these chills." They left me at once. She told me to sit up when I chose, and to eat whatever I wanted. My babe was born about two o'clock in the morning, and the following evening I sat up for several hours. I ate whatever the family did. I had a boiled dinner of meat and vegetables the second day. I made no difference in my diet, except to drink gruel between meals, and never experienced the least inconvenience from this course. I dressed myself the second day, and the third day felt unwilling to lie down. In one week I was about the house and was well, running up and down stairs and attending to domestic duties. For several years I had been troubled with prolapsus uteri, which disappeared entirely after Mrs. Eddy's wonderful demonstration of Christian Science at the birth of my babe.[12]

S. P. Bancroft, also a student at that period, has written that Mrs. Glover was "absolutely fearless" in the presence of sickness, and lenient with those who "erred through ignorance," but that she "suffered intensely" from a belief that her work was being retarded by some of those who had taken from her teaching only the doctrine of mind's control over matter without differentiating between the divine Mind and the carnal mind which is "enmity against God" and "a murderer from the beginning."

The anguish of some of her letters during this period shows how keenly she felt the burden of students clinging to her mentally for help or else opening their minds to the venomous whispers that were being circulated by some of her former students. In her work *Rudimental Divine Science,* published many years later, she wrote: "The Discoverer of this Science could tell you of timidity, of self-distrust, of friendlessness, toil, agonies, and victories under which she needed miraculous vision to sustain her, when taking the first footsteps in this Science." When one looks at the turbulence and uncertainties that beset her in those days as she explored the strange new world of mental forces opened up to her by her discovery, the word "miraculous" does not seem

---

[12] Quoted in 16th edition of *Science and Health,* p. 179 f.

extravagant. For in the midst of it all she was able to go on healing, teaching, inspiring, and strengthening her students, lavishing on them those qualities which Bancroft, in his reminiscences, refers to as "her humanity, her tenderness, her graciousness, her appreciation of little attentions shown her."

Something of the cost of all this is hinted at in a letter written by Bancroft to Mary Beecher Longyear many decades later. Describing Mrs. Glover's appearance at the time he first knew her, he speaks of her eyes—"dark blue with a wonderful lustre, but sad, very sad at times, yet with a glory shining through." In those days, he explains, he could not understand this luminous appearance of the eyes, on which so many of her contemporaries commented; but he adds: "I can see now it was the shining through of soul, a striving to give birth to secrets of great moment, while lamenting over the unwillingness of those whom she loved to receive her message. And yet her vision was clear; it could look forward to the glorious consummations of the future." And for all the sadness that her experience may have brought her, there was a deep-running current of joy evident in her life, and even a recurrent gaiety. Bancroft adds: "I should say she was naturally joy-loving and light-hearted." In the same vein Fisher was to write: "Though she walked over thorns, her tread was as light as air."

It was on the first day of 1877 that, to the utter surprise of her other students, she married Gilbert Eddy. She had found a strong right arm to assist her in the work, and it must have seemed to her that the best way to calm the welter of jealousies and cross-purposes around her was to accept the offer of marriage from this man on whose faithful love and devotion she already counted so heavily. There was a subsequent period of calm, but in March, 1877, George Barry brought suit against her for $2700 as payment for the services he had rendered her during his five years of discipleship, and obtained an attachment on her house.

About this time, with this new harassment threatening, her thought turned again to Alcott. She wired him an invitation to attend the meeting of her next class, and received from him a friendly but vague reply:

DEAR MRS. EDDY,

Your telegram came quite unseasonably for me to respond on my return from Boston yesterday, and I cannot conveniently leave again today to meet yourself and Class as it would have been pleasant for me to have done. I have hoped to see you in Concord sometime for further conversation. And Mrs. Emerson once expressed her wish to meet you.

Now that spring approaches perhaps you will avail yourself of some fine day to look in upon us, with your husband, to whom, with yourself

my respectful compliments
A. BRONSON ALCOTT

There was not much encouragement in the invitation for "some fine day," but in August we find Alcott noting in his journal: "Write to Mrs. Eddy of Lynn, whose book *Science and Health* is one of the hopeful signs of the times. Mrs. E. wishes to visit us and meet Mr. and Mrs. Emerson." The letter itself makes no mention of the Emersons: "I have wished to make your visit here every way agreeable to you. But fear it would be disappointing to you during this week. My daughter Louisa is just now quite unable to entertain company, and my wife is mostly confined to her chamber. Still, if you think it worth the while to come up and see *me*, I shall gladly meet you. I regret the circumstances, but am none the less interested in yourself and your views."

The visit evidently did not take place, but several weeks later, when George Barry's suit was about to come up in court, Mrs. Eddy again wrote him. Alcott notes in his journal: "Write to Mrs. Eddy of Lynn, declining to visit her at this time for conversation on health, etc. The good lady has wholesome views upon health and healing. A former visit of mine impressed me favorably regarding her methods, and especially her faith in spiritual as distinguished from the sorceries of current spiritualism, fast running its polluting social race into detestation." The letter he wrote was courteous but preoccupied, and was once more vague as to future meetings: "On returning from a visit to Connecticut I find your kind letter inviting me to visit you at Lynn. It is now too late and besides I cannot well at present leave home, having been called from Connecticut by Mrs. Alcott's illness. She is now more comfortable, but still requires our attendance. I may hope at some future time to have the pleasure of an interview."

Shortly afterward the Barry case came up in court, and the embittered young man was awarded $350 instead of the $2700 he asked. More importantly, the case marked a final break between Mrs. Eddy and Spofford, her former right-hand man, who on this occasion testified on behalf of Barry.

Dissension over the financing and publicizing of *Science and Health* as well as resentment at the growing importance of the part played by Gilbert Eddy, form the background of the Spofford defection. Mrs. Eddy, profoundly certain that she was acting under the divine Mind's direction, saw these outward symptoms as indications of that deeper "criminal" or "animal" instinct of mortal mind which would, if undetected and undestroyed, use even the most guileless of persons to block the progress of Christian Science. The day before she married Gilbert Eddy she had written to Spofford, foreshadowing the later decisive break:

No student or mortal has tried to have you leave me that I know of. Dr. Eddy has tried to have you stay. You are in a mistake; it is God and not man who has separated us and for the reason I begin to learn. Do not think of returning to me again. . . . God produces the separation and I submit to it. So must you. There is no cloud between us, but the way you set me up for a Dagon is wrong, and now I implore you to return forever from this error of personality and go alone to God as I have taught you.

So Spofford departed to join the ranks of those whom Mrs. Eddy denominated as "mesmerists," and an energetic young Prussian cabinetmaker named Edward J. Arens moved in to a position of considerable prominence in the little group. Possessed of a passion for litigation, Arens argued forcefully that it was only right and just that various "disloyal" students should be made to honor certain financial obligations they had toward her, and a small rash of lawsuits accordingly broke out in the months following the Barry case. This is by all odds the period in the history of Christian Science farthest removed from its present-day atmosphere, but from it Mrs. Eddy evidently drew invaluable lessons.

In the midst of it she again wrote to Alcott. It is not clear what her specific request was, but apparently she hoped to find in him an understanding of the almost overwhelming problems she was facing. Her letter arrived, however, at an inopportune moment. On November 17 Alcott wrote her:

Your appeal to me for assistance in the matter of your court trial, touches me deeply; and I wish it were in my power to give you my presence as well as sympathy and to further if I might the cause of justice. But my wife is now passing from us, and I may not leave her for a night, hardly for a day dutifully.

Under these circumstances I trust you will excuse me from giving further attention to your affairs at present. If you are wronged those who have been dishonest though they may contrive to get the decree of Courts in their favor, will ultimately suffer the penalties of their misdeeds, and you will be justified, not only to your own heart, but before the law also.

A week later Mrs. Alcott died, a heroine in her own right, the courageous supporter and long-suffering victim of her husband's gentle impracticality. Cyrus Bartol, that other indestructible Transcendentalist still preaching in Boston, paid tribute at the funeral to her noble character, and William Lloyd Garrison followed with reminiscences of her and her "saintly brother," Samuel J. May, while Emerson sat inarticulately beside his grief-stricken, lifelong friend. More than miles separated the fading, sunset world of Concord from the storm-tossed little group in Lynn.

But six months later Lynn suddenly presented itself at Concord in the person of Gilbert Eddy. On May 12, 1878, Alcott noted in his journal:

> Mr. Eddy of Lynn comes and urges me to accompany him home and witness a "trial for sorcery" to be held before the Supreme Judicial Court tomorrow at Salem. A student of Mrs. Eddy's is accused of debasing his art of healing, and is prosecuted by the patient for this abuse.
>
> Mrs. Eddy is the author of a work entitled *Science and Health*, in which she sets forth the principles and method of sympathetic healing. She has a school of disciples. I have some reference to herself and work in my Diaries, having once made her a visit and met her classes.

This was the sensational culmination of the period of litigation engineered by Arens. The Boston papers were hailing it as a modern "Salem witchcraft trial." The apostate student charged with exercising his mesmeric powers to cause the plaintiff (one Lucretia Brown of Ipswich, Massachusetts) great suffering of mind and body was none other than Daniel Harrison Spofford, who had received Alcott on his second visit to Lynn (which now apparently had merged with his first visit in the old man's memory).

It would seem a tribute both to Gilbert Eddy's powers of earnest persuasion and to Bronson Alcott's fund of luminous sympathy that the aged Transcendentalist should have consented to be drawn, even momentarily, into this unhappy affair. It was apparently on this occasion that he said to Mrs. Eddy the words which she recalled with gratitude years later: "I have come to comfort you." In his journal the next day he simply wrote: "Accompany Mr. and Mrs. Eddy to Salem. Judge Gray, on opening the Court, entertains the case and names Friday next for a hearing. The young lady plaintiff is present, and has no question of the sorcery practised upon her, to the detriment of her health and reason."

The reserve of the entry speaks eloquently. Alcott could hardly have had any understanding of the whirlpool of mental influences into which Mrs. Eddy's little group had been launched by their daring venture beyond all the known boundaries of the mind-matter relationship. Emerson had written years before: "How slowly, how slowly we learn that witchcraft and ghostcraft, palmistry and magic, and all the other so-called superstitions, which, with so much police, boastful skepticism, and scientific committees, we had finally dismissed to the moon as nonsense, are really no nonsense at all, but subtle and valid influences, always starting up, mowing, muttering in our path, and shading our day." But this was metaphor only. A quarter of a century was to pass before Hugo Münsterberg, then head of the Department of Psychology at Harvard, was seriously to investigate the possible connections of hypnotism and crime, and half a century more before a case arose in Denmark in which, a hypnotized subject having robbed a bank and killed two men during the robbery, the subject was sentenced to two years in prison but the hypnotist was given life. Charcot was just beginning to show in Paris, through experiments on hypnotized patients, that "hysterical paralysis" could be first caused and then cured by suggestion; and only after two more generations of experimentation were a few adventurous psychoanalysts, notably Jan Ehrenwald in his *New Dimensions of Deep Analysis*, to explore cautiously the possibility of telepathic influences between analyst and patient quite apart from hypnosis—a possibility having implications far beyond the trivial examples Ehrenwald adduces.

Viewed in such a perspective, the trial at Salem may be accounted as registering the first rude shock of awareness of criminal possibilities in the use of suggestion—possibilities utterly ruled out by the method of Christian Science, with its sharp line of distinction between God's will and erring human will power and its emphasis on Paul's command to "Let this mind be in you, which was also in Christ Jesus." The suit itself was hardly an effective example of Christian method. Mrs. Eddy, according to her own statement, was vigorously opposed to its being brought, and she was particularly amazed to hear the plaintiff's claim that she was helpless to defend herself against Spofford's baleful mental influence. Such a claim was a direct contradiction of the teaching of Christian Science, which rested on the superiority of the divine Mind to every form of specious mind-power. Telepathy, hypnosis, and all those occult influences which Emerson described as "subtle and valid" must inevitably lose all claim to validity in the clear light of spiritual understanding. Whatever disturbing phases Mrs. Eddy's mental explorations might be carrying her through, that innermost conviction of the total reality of Spirit's pure, inviolable universe of good never left her; it constituted the tranquil center at the heart of the storm.

Here we may find an explanation of her turning to Alcott on this occasion. Essentially she stood alone, supported only by her unshakable assurance of God's direction in bringing to the world the great illumination that had dawned on her. For the most part the world remained indifferent or hostile to this gift which was meant for the healing of its ills. Even her students seemed unable to grasp the fullness of her vision. She was to write later of her task "of continual recapitulation of tired aphorisms and disappointed ethics; of patching breaches widened the next hour; of pounding wisdom and love into sounding brass; of warming marble and quenching volcanoes!" At such a volcanic moment as the present, Alcott's serenity and sanity must have stood in welcome contrast to the agitations and alarms of those students who persistently misunderstood her teachings about "malicious animal magnetism." Yet if she hoped for a deeper comprehension of the situation from him, she was due to be disappointed. He might lend his sympathetic presence, but he showed no sign of recognizing that these were apocalyptic struggles in which the little group was engaged.

Nevertheless, the visit went off better than might have been expected. On this same occasion, in addition to the trip to Salem, she took Alcott to call on a Unitarian minister, Samuel B. Stewart, who was an old acquaintance of his and whom she had known since coming to Lynn in 1870. This social visit was evidently a casual, equable affair, which Stewart recalled many years later with pleasure, and it suggests the reserves of equanimity on which she could draw even in the midst of such extraordinary events.

On the following Friday the case came up in court without benefit of Alcott's presence. Spofford's attorney filed a demurrer, which the presiding judge immediately sustained. It was not within the power of the court, he ruled, to restrain Mr. Spofford's mind. And so the whole bizarre episode came to an anticlimactic close.

3.

There had never been any real possibility of Alcott's and Mrs. Eddy's having a merely casual friendship. The dynamics of the new movement had no place for an idealism that stayed at the conversational level, and Mrs. Eddy's attempt to reach through to Alcott at a point of crucial understanding had met with placid incomprehension. Three weeks later a final visit is recorded, this time in Boston:

> I take tea with Dr. Dudley at his boardings in Worcester Square, and after tea we meet Mrs. Eddy and her class of students at Mrs. Frothingham's parlors in West Newton Street. The party consists of fifteen or more young gentlemen and ladies preparing to become healers of disease by Mrs. Eddy's theory. They call themselves "Christian Scientists," and their method the "Mental Method."
>
> I have but an imperfect acquaintance with this theory of healing, and infer that she may have skill to remove, perhaps cure, some of the nervous maladies incident to improper modes of diet, both of body and mind. There is perhaps a touch of fanaticism, though of a genial quality, interposed into her faith, which a deeper insight into the mysteries of life may ultimately remove. I judge her present gifts are rather derived from her nervous temperament, combined with the faith with which she ventures into hitherto unexplored crypts of psychology, than from any established philosophy concerning such recondite matters.
>
> But any touch of idealism, however dashed with superstition, over-clouded with mysticism, is to be regarded as a wholesome omen in these times of shallow materialism and atheistic dogmatism, in which so many indulge.

This is Alcott's—one might almost say Transcendentalism's —final judgment on Christian Science. The skeptic, judging only by some of the outward circumstances at the time, may feel that it is a very generous estimate. The Christian Scientist, looking at the inwardness of Mrs. Eddy's vision and its fruits in his own life and thought, may feel that it measures Transcendentalism's inability to break away, at the crucial point, from the worldly view of those to whom matter is the basic reality.

Here is Alcott, early in the history of the new movement, adopting the convenient explanation that has been resorted to a thousand times since: Christian Science may be able to cure "nervous maladies" in a haphazard sort of way, but such limited empirical achievements do not come from any "established philosophy." To the materialist any other conclusion is ruled out *a priori*—even if, strictly speaking, his philosophy does not allow for *a priori* judgments. Alcott, of course, was not a materialist, but in the eyes of Christian Scientists his idealism is tainted with what might be called the ultimate refinement of materialism, a sort of homeopathic attenuation of it to the point where matter very nearly disappears as a component of absolute reality but remains as a necessary limitation on the power of Spirit. Here Alcott himself shows that "common sense" which Emerson considered the mark of all valid minds and which he defined as the perception of matter or, more broadly, the recognition of the limiting circumstance, the historical fact.

This point throws light on the contention made by Woodbridge Riley that Alcott is one of the major sources of Christian Science doctrine. Mrs. Eddy, Riley held, must have read some of Alcott's published works while she was writing *Science and Health* and must have included some of his basic ideas, in a debased and misunderstood form, in that book. Riley cites what he imagines to be parallel passages, though by any serious critical standards they show only the vaguest analogy. Some of the passages from Transcendental writers quoted in the first chapter of this book offer far more striking parallels. Riley, incidentally, with characteristic slovenliness fails to note the two points at which Alcott's philosophy and Christian Science really do meet: in the doctrines of pre-existence and of man as "including the universe."

But a great gulf divides Christian Science from all forms of Transcendentalism. It occurs at the point where Mrs. Eddy's teaching departs entirely from Emersonian "common sense," the point at which it denies all reality to matter. Berkeley could preserve matter as at least an idea in the mind of God, and Alcott in a sort of Hindu-cum-Hegel fashion could allow for it in his concept of the Not-One to which the One is constantly giving birth. Riley himself concedes the distinction between Alcott and Christian Science on this point:

> Alcott as an idealist might say, and did say, that there was no matter in mind, but he could not say that there was no mind in matter. He was an idealist, but not an illusionist. Matter to him was real, but only in the sense of a far-flung emanation of spirit, the outermost ring thrown off from the central source of spiritual light. This made matter in a sense a shadow projected by spirit across space; it did not make it a phantom, an absolute unreality, "an error of mortal mind."

The point can be made crystal clear by a passage from Alcott's journal written in the *annus mirabilis* of 1836. It reads in part:

> I fancy that the hour is coming when all that moved in the mind of Jesus and prompted those sublime ideas on the soul's origin and immortality—that exposed nature and mastered its synthesis, that knew men and prescribed the healing of the human body as well as the soul—that all this shall come out as an actual distinct idea in the mind. I imagine that it will be possible, yea, certain, that the miracles, so called, wrought out by this faith in the spiritual and apprehension of the material,

shall be made as common facts, the necessary and natural results of spiritual laws.

Taken by themselves, these words might almost seem a literal prophecy of Christian Science, but put in their context they indicate a vastly different philosophical starting point. The sentences preceding and succeeding the quoted passage read:

I am now finding an interest in the phenomena of the external world. I have a desire to apprehend the laws of which these phenomena are the pledge and appearance. This embraces the science of physiology. I have a dim yet assured instinct that these laws, when viewed from their true point in the vision of Spirit, will appear much more than has generally been supposed. . . . The study of organs and functions will, I apprehend, become but another view of the Spirit's activity in body. Physiology is none other than the study of Spirit incarnate. We must wed the science of physiology and psychology, and from these shall spring the Divine Idea which, originally one in the mind of God, He saw fit to separate and spread throughout his twofold creation.

This passage helps to explain Alcott's almost obsessive interest in dietary theory, an interest which relates him more to Gandhi than to the Teacher who said, "Take no thought for your life, what ye shall eat . . ." More basically, its underlying concept of a "twofold creation" opposes it sharply to the fundamental conviction of Christian Science that there is but one creation, which is wholly spiritual. To Christian Scientists this conviction is all-important. It is, they hold, the heart of the "revelation" that came to Mrs. Eddy in 1866. It conclusively separates Christian Science from all forms of "mind cure," which may more properly be derived from Quimby's doctrine of mind-over-matter. It gives to the terms that Christian Science shares with Transcendentalism a new metaphysical content and a more concrete applicability.

Take the term "Father-Mother God." Mrs. Eddy was by no means the first to use this phrase or concept. But earlier users, despite their theoretical or poetic concept of it, had all conceived of man as a spiritual being clothed, at least temporarily, in clay. Thus he was, in effect, the child of a Father God and a Mother Nature, whereas Christian Science held him to be in reality wholly spiritual because he was the child of a Father-Mother who was wholly Spirit. The mortal offspring was not to be considered the child of God—not even the "fallen" child of God. He was only the imperfect, finite concept of the child of God held by that supposititious consciousness termed mortal mind.

This, in turn, separated Christian Science from Alcott's central doctrine of Lapse—the Oriental-Neoplatonic theory which finds its orthodox Christian counterpart in the Adamic "fall of man." Mrs. Eddy totally rejected this traditional position. Consequently she was enabled to accept Darwinism as a plausible hypothesis of the stages through which mortal mind's conception of reality has passed. It is a striking fact that in 1875, when orthodox Christianity was protesting in outrage against the new theory of evolution, Mrs. Eddy stated calmly in the first edition of *Science and Health*: "Mr. Darwin is right with regard to mortal man or matter, but should have made a distinction between these and the immortal, whose basis is Spirit." [13] And again, she spoke of matter as a grosser substratum of mortal mind, "wherein one belief introduces and destroys another in Darwinian process." The Eden myth she took purely as an allegory of the supposed rise of man from "the dust of the ground" and the inevitable condemnation of that false concept of man to ultimate annihilation.

[13] In later editions this statement was altered to allow for the modifications of biological theory which have since taken place. Her final edition of *Science and Health* asked, with appropriate scientific caution, "May not Darwin be right . . . ?"

It is right here that we confront the basic philosophical question raised by Christian Science. In a perfect, spiritual universe created by a perfect, infinite Mind, how could a false concept of creation ever arise or even *seem* to arise?

Mrs. Eddy was well aware of the problem. She repeatedly referred to human existence as an "enigma." [14] If there were a rational answer to the enigma, if the mortal illusion could be "explained," then evil or error would have a rational place in the universe, it would be a part of the divine perfection. And to that proposition Mrs. Eddy gave an uncompromising "No!"

Catholicism, with the help of Plato out of Boethius, had for centuries taught the "unreality" of evil in a philosophical sense. Leibniz and Spinoza, and after them Edwards, had brought their massive intellectual powers to absolve cosmic perfection of that which finite minds call evil. Yet particular evils remained, and the anguished sufferer could still cry out against the injustice of the terrible and incomprehensible Power whose "good" contained such fiendish cruelties. Was this indeed the heavenly Father of whom the compassionate Healer of Galilee had said: "He that hath seen me hath seen the Father"? Were these dialectical solutions of the problem of evil an adequate substitute for the dynamic revelation of reality that took place when Jesus said with

---

[14] Cf. Tillich's attitude to the "existential question." Man's existential predicament, as opposed to his essential nature as the image of God, may be analyzed by the philosopher, says Tillich, but the question it raises can be answered only on the basis of a tradition drawn from something other than the human situation or existential predicament itself. At another level of perception Sir James Jeans stated that "the physicist can warn the philosopher that no *intelligible* interpretation of the workings of nature is to be expected," and P. W. Bridgman similarly wrote of the modern physicist's realization "that the structure of nature may eventually be such that our processes of thought do not correspond to it sufficiently to permit us to think about it at all." Like the existentialist, the physicist can accept logical absurdity as in the nature of material existence.

authority: "Receive thy sight. . . . Rise up and walk. . . . Be whole"?

Hume in the eighteenth century had repeated the three questions of Epicurus about God: "Is he willing to prevent evil, but not able? then is he impotent. Is he able, but not willing? then is he malevolent. Is he both able and willing? whence then is evil?" Calvinism had frankly taken the second position, and, for all its vision of God's majesty, it held Him responsible for creating a human race which He knew from the outset would end in damnation. Protestant liberalism essentially took the first position, and, for all its vision of God's love, it held Him dependent on the good will and reason of a fallible human race for the realization of His beneficent purposes. Alone in all history—unless one accepts her contention that this was the very answer Christ gave—Mrs. Eddy replied that evil is literally and demonstrably *nothing*.

In one of her profoundest short works, *Unity of Good,* she was to write:

> What is the cardinal point of the difference in my metaphysical system? This: that *by knowing the unreality of disease, sin, and death,* you demonstrate the allness of God. This difference wholly separates my system from all others. The reality of these so-called existences I deny, because they are not to be found in God, and this system is built on Him as the sole cause. It would be difficult to name any previous teachers, save Jesus and his apostles, who have thus taught.

Her answer to the problem of evil was, then, not an argument but a fact, a practical "demonstration." Hence the crucial part played in her system by healing—as contemporary theology is increasingly admitting it plays a crucial part in the New Testament. Confronted by a particular evil, it was useless for the individual to ask: "Where has this evil come from? How can it present itself to me, even as an illusion? Does not its presence indicate that God at least permits it, if He does not send it?" Instead, one needed to recognize the evil as without cause, reason, legitimacy, permanence, or power. One needed to recognize oneself as the manifestation of infinite Mind, incapable of accepting illusion as reality. One needed, above all, to recognize the immutable perfection of Mind's spiritual creation, which could not possibly permit the presence of anything contrary to its own nature. And the result of such yielding to the divine Mind must inevitably be healing, a radical changing of the evidence before the senses.

For all his open-mindedness, this was too bold a leap for Alcott to take. If he himself had experienced a sudden, overwhelming, quite "miraculous" healing, it might have been different. Then he might have found himself catapulted by that experience across what appeared to be a logical gap in the new teaching to a point from which he could think *down* into limited human experience with unbroken logic instead of up from it. Mrs. Eddy herself recognized the need for the concrete demonstration of healing as a step in apprehending her purely deductive system when she wrote: "Christian Science must be accepted at this period by induction. We admit the whole, because a part is proved and that part illustrates and proves the entire Principle."

From the radical vantage point afforded by such a Principle one could ask questions and pose dilemmas quite as embarrassing to traditional idealism as the old problem raised by Epicurus. It was easier for Alcott to assume that what Mrs. Eddy needed was "a deeper insight into the mysteries of life" than it would have been for him to face unflinchingly the question she posed in *Science and Health* for all who would build on Spirit *and* matter:

When we endow matter with vague spiritual power,—that is, when we do so in our theories, for of course we cannot really endow matter with what it does not and cannot possess,— we disown the Almighty, for such theories lead to one of two things. They either presuppose the self-evolution and self-government of matter, or else they assume that matter is the product of Spirit. To seize the first horn of the dilemma and consider matter as a power in and of itself, is to leave the creator out of His own universe; while to grasp the other horn of the dilemma and regard God as the creator of matter, is not only to make Him responsible for all disasters, physical and moral, but to announce Him as their source, thereby making Him guilty of maintaining perpetual misrule in the form and under the name of natural law.

But it was evident, by the time he paid this last visit to Mrs. Eddy, that Alcott had missed the essential logic of her position. It may even be that he unconsciously resented a little her insistent emphasis on healing, since this accepted a challenge which his own philosophy had vaguely glimpsed but had never attempted to meet. It was easier to go along with the general skepticism as to her having anything very remarkable to show in that direction. For that matter, didn't she herself have to wear spectacles for reading? (He could not know that she would finally be healed of this when she was over seventy, and read fine print with ease in her ninetieth year.) [15] Then, too, wonderfully hospitable though he was to new ideas, his own brilliant Neoplatonic synthesis was not easily to be modified in this his seventy-ninth year. On this very occasion, he told Mrs. Eddy's class about *his* ideas, and the official minutes of the meeting read: "After listening to questions & answers between teacher and class, Mr. Alcott presented his argument of the working of mind

---

[15] See *What Mrs. Eddy Said to Arthur Brisbane* (New York, M. E. Paige, 1930), p. 53.

from Spirit down to atom & 'vice versa.' It was interesting to notice how near some points in the argument approached to the true argument in Science."

Yes, it was and is interesting to see how closely the two approached, and how unbridgeably far apart they remained. When the tedious archangel and the "fair saint"—who had now faded in Alcott's eyes to a genial fanatic—parted at Mrs. Frothingham's parlors in West Newton Street that day, it was clear that the basic difference between Transcendentalism and Christian Science was incomparably more important than any superficial likeness; and the parting was permanent.

The very next year, 1879, Alcott was to see the realization of a lifelong dream in the formation of the Concord School of Philosophy, from which, he was sure, fresh currents of Platonic idealism would flow out across the continent and transform the face of American life. And at almost identically the same moment twenty-six students of Mrs. Eddy met with their teacher to form the Church of Christ, Scientist, as an institution "designed to commemorate the word and works of our Master, which should reinstate primitive Christianity and its lost element of healing."

4.

To the Summer School at Concord came pilgrims from all over the country. Alcott, as dean of the school, presided with grace and ability. Some of the older Transcendentalists like Bartol and Hedge participated in the sessions, as well as a later crop from the Middle West; and new, vigorous figures like James and Royce lent their presence. Here, surely, was a bridge to another Golden Age.

The Boston press, naturally enough, made merry with the erudite goings-on in the little Hillside Chapel. Stories circulated that the philosophers discussed such things as "the whatness of the howsoever" and "the thingness of the why." Equally burlesque was the summing up of the lectures in two questions and answers: "What's mind? No matter. What's matter? Never mind." Yet there was good teaching and profound thinking that took place at the sessions; if the school looks a little pathetic in retrospect, it was far from being contemptible, as critics then and now have painted it. It was Transcendentalism's own Indian summer, but it served as a reminder in a pragmatic society of the vital warmth of ideas.

A young Episcopal clergyman, Andrew J. Graham, who attended in 1881, wrote fifty-seven years later—many years after he had left the Episcopal Church to become a Christian Science practitioner, teacher, and lecturer—that he still visited Hillside Chapel two or three times a year, not in a mood of sad reminiscence, but of "present enjoyment," implying that the values gained there had kept pace with him through a lifetime. He spoke also of sharing his vivid appreciation of the school with the aged Lilian Whiting, who, as an ebullient young journalist from the West in 1881, had reported the sessions in the Boston *Traveler* with such a glow of enthusiasm that even Bronson Alcott was a little taken aback.

What really disturbed the latter, however, was the way in which the influence of Hegel gradually rode down that of Plato in the academy. However much he might deplore the "purely speculative," it won the day. The resounding success of William T. Harris, the St. Louis Hegelian, finally caused Hiram K. Jones, the Platonist from Jacksonville, Illinois, who had been co-founder of the school with Alcott, to withdraw from it altogether. The dream of a new Platonic Academy seemed to fade before the intellectual onslaught of high-powered German metaphysics. Though the sessions continued until 1889, there was a gradual decline of enthusiasm and unity after 1882.

That was a momentous year in other ways for Alcott. In April Emerson died. For almost fifty years the two men had been bound together in a deep though elusive intimacy. As a young man, Alcott had played Socrates to Emerson's Plato; and as an old man, he had counted more than he knew on his old friend's cool and discerning affection. As Emerson's memory gave way in his last years and his powers waned, the two understood each other even when words failed. After his last visit to his friend's sickbed, Alcott described in his journal how Emerson turned "his kind glance, smiling as none other, upon me," but "seemed confused, and uttered words too indistinctly to be discerned," then "took my hand affectionately and said in strong but broken accents: 'You have strong hold on life, and maintain it firmly,' when his voice faltered and fell into indistinctness." And so Emerson himself drifted off into the last indistinctness, with something pure and silver still shining as the mist closed in.

His Swedenborgian friend, Henry James the elder, who died in the same year, noted affectionately that quality of indistinctness, of something not quite focused, which had attended his genius from the start. "Mr. Emerson," he wrote, ". . . was an American John the Baptist, proclaiming tidings of great joy to the American Israel; but, like John the Baptist, he could so little foretell the form in which the predicted good was to appear, that when you went to him he was always uncertain whether you were he who should come, or another."

In this connection, a curious incident occurred some months before his death. Mrs. Eddy "went to him." Without benefit of Alcott as intermediary, she realized her long-held desire to meet the Sage of Concord. In an undated letter to an unidentified Miss Lane of Chicago, she wrote:

Waldo Emerson was a man fitting a nich in history well, and we all in Mass. love him. But he was as far from accepting Christian Science as a man can be who is a strict moralist. Bronson Alcott is far in advance of him. I saw Emerson some months before his demise; went for the purpose of *healing* him. Let no one but my husband, Dr. Eddy, who went with me, know it. As soon as I got into the deep recesses of his thoughts I saw his case was hopeless. I can work only by God's graces and by His rules. So when I said, in reply to his remark, "I am old and my brains are wearing out from hard labor," —and then chattered like a babe,— "But you believe in the powers of God above all other causation, do you not?" He answered, "Yes," and this followed in substance: but it would be profane for me to believe a man does not wear out. I don't believe God can or wants to prevent this result of old age.

Sixteen years earlier, in the very year in which Mrs. Eddy had had her overwhelming revelation of "Life in and of Spirit; this Life being the sole reality of existence," Emerson had prepared for the decline to come in his poem "Terminus":

> It is time to be old,
> To take in sail:—
> The god of bounds,
> Who sets to seas a shore,
> Came to me in his fatal rounds,
> And said: "No more! . . ."

This was a far cry from the brave words he had written as a younger man: "This old age ought not to creep on a human mind. I see no need of it. Whilst we converse with what is above us, we do not grow old, but grow young." And again: "Is it possible a man should not grow old? I will not answer for this crazy body. It seems a ship which carries him through the waves of this world and whose timbers contract barnacles and dry rot, and will not serve for a second course. But I refuse to admit this appeal to the old people we know as valid against a good hope. For do we know one who is an organ of the Holy Ghost?" Or the sharp cry of protest: "This old age; this ossification of the heart; this fat in the brain; this degeneracy; is the Fall of Man."

Those boundless, radical hopes and protests, challenging the very structure of the brute world of the senses, had given way to the undemanding optimism which accepted the limitations of the natural world as necessary and beneficent parts of the divine plan. The first lesson of history, said Emerson in this acquiescent mood, is the good of that which men call evil. It is this phase of his thinking of which Santayana was to write in his *Interpretations of Poetry and Religion* (New York, Charles Scribner's Sons, 1911) p. 228:

> There is evil, of course, he tells us. Experience is sad. There is a crack in everything that God has made. But, ah! the laws of the universe are sacred and beneficent. Without them nothing good could arise. All things, then, are in their right places and the universe is perfect above our querulous tears. Perfect? we may ask. But perfect from what point of view, in reference to what ideal? To its own? To that of a man who renouncing himself and all naturally dear to him, ignoring the injustice, suffering, and impotence in the world, allows his will and his conscience to be hypnotized by the spectacle of a necessary evolution, and lulled into cruelty by the pomp and music of a tragic show? In that case the evil is not explained, it is forgotten; it is not cured, but condoned.

Mrs. Eddy was not given to this sort of delicately worded and intellectually sophisticated analysis, but in her brief comment on her talk with Emerson she went to the heart of the matter. Recognizing the moral purity which characterized both Emerson's idealism and Christian Science,[16]

---

[16] Cf. her statement in 1903: "Far be it from me to tread on the ashes of the dead or to dissever any unity that may exist between Christian Science

she nevertheless saw his optimistic acquiescence in the natural order of the sense-world—which, from a more worldly point of view, might be accounted the ripe wisdom of experience—as "hopeless" from her own standpoint of limitless challenge. Certainly Alcott, as well as the earlier Emerson, was closer to her vision of reality. Yet neither of them had ever been ready to reject the entire complex of material appearances as a misconception of reality, as she demanded.

Pointing out how evil seeks "to fasten all error upon God, and so make the lie seem part of eternal Truth," she wrote some years later:

> Emerson says, "Hitch your wagon to a star." I say, Be allied to the deific power, and all that is good will aid your journey, as the stars in their courses fought against Sisera. . . . Hourly, in Christian Science, man thus weds himself with God, or rather he ratifies a union thus predestined from all eternity; but evil ties its wagon-load of offal to the divine chariots,—or seeks so to do,—that its vileness may be christened purity, and its darkness get consolation from borrowed scintillations.

If this seems unduly harsh on Emerson, it is no harsher than history in the twentieth century has been on his optimistic acceptance of "the good of evil." The theory that the mass extermination of six million Jews by Hitler, for instance, was part of the lovely workings of a benign universe can be argued intellectually, but we have learned to ask to what extent such intellectual solutions of the problem of evil may paralyze—or "hypnotize"—the will and conscience.

To the founder of Christian Science the vital distinction lay between an intellectual and a spiritual denial of evil,

---

and the philosophy of a great and good man, for such was Ralph Waldo Emerson. . . . Human merit or demerit will find its proper level. Divinity alone solves the problem of humanity, and that in God's own time. 'By their fruits ye shall know them.' " (*The First Church of Christ, Scientist, and Miscellany*, p. 306.)

the one leaving it as necessary illusion, the other attacking it as illegitimate fraud. A student of hers, Hanover P. Smith, whom she had healed of deafness and dumbness, published in 1886 an exuberant little pamphlet entitled *Writings and Genius of the Founder of Christian Science,* in which he drew that very distinction. "At times," he wrote, "we can see that Plato and Emerson caught glimpses of the Soul-principle; but they never retained the vision long enough to let go the intellectual view and see spiritually." And Mrs. Eddy wrote on the flyleaf of her own copy of *Nature:* "Emerson put so much reason into Mind and so much philosophy into Science that he lost the true sense of Spirit, God." [17]

One is reminded by all this of Emerson's own comment on Plato:

> He is intellectual in his aim; and therefore in expression literary, mounting into heaven, diving into the pit, expounding the laws of the state, the passion of love, the remorse of crime, the hope of the parting soul—he is literary and never otherwise. It is almost the sole deduction from the merit of Plato that his writings have not—what is no doubt incident to this regnancy of intellect in his work—the vital authority which the screams of prophets and the sermons of unlettered Arabs and Jews possess. There is an interval; and to cohesion contact is necessary.

It might be summed up in Augustine's percipient statement that despite all the splendid things he found in Plato, he nowhere found the words: "Come unto me, all ye that labour and are heavy laden, and I will give you rest."

Even Alcott, who was so much more of a doer than Emerson and whose link with historic Christianity was so much closer, comes under the shadow of this judgment. "My debt to Plato," he wrote, "is greater, perhaps, than to any mind—

---

[17] It is worth noting that she told one of her secretaries that she had not read any Emerson until after writing *Science and Health.* (Powell, *Mary Baker Eddy: A Life Size Portrait,* p. 131.)

greater than to Christ, I sometimes think, whose spirit is an element of humanity but whose genius I did not entertain and comprehend till Plato unsealed my eyes and led me to the study of his fair performance." Perhaps Alcott may safely be left halfway between Emerson and Mrs. Eddy.

In October of 1882, six months after the death of his friend, Alcott suffered an apoplectic stroke. Though he learned to walk and talk once more, he was never again able to write. For a few years he lingered on, presiding still over the summer sessions of the Concord School, spending long hours re-reading his journals, looking back quietly over a lifetime of dreams and hopes. It was a beautiful last chapter, full of gentle luster, and it has been exquisitely recorded by Odell Shepard.

In 1888 he passed away, two days before his daughter Louisa. Transcendentalism's Indian summer was over. Before 1892 the Plato Club, the American Akademe, the Philosophical Society, the Concord School of Philosophy, the *Journal of Speculative Philosophy* came to an end. The dream was all but forgotten, and the nation rushed on toward the glittering goal of material success.

5.

But Christian Science was not being forgotten! The year 1882 opened a new chapter for Mrs. Eddy, too. Her experience of the malicious opposition of the "carnal mind" seemed to culminate in that year with the death of Gilbert Eddy from heart disease, brought on perhaps by his burdened sense of struggling with "the enemy"—the most recent manifestation of which was the opposition of the aggressive and now apostate Mr. Arens. His death was not only a deep personal loss to Mrs. Eddy, as her letters of the period show poignantly, but a severe challenge to the movement. Yet from it she rose triumphantly to press forward with immeasurably greater success than before and with a new confidence in the supremacy of Truth forged out of the bitter lessons of the past.

For several weeks following Gilbert Eddy's passing, she stayed in Vermont in the home of Arthur True Buswell, one of her students, and an account based on his reminiscences tells of the impression she made on the two or three students with her at the time: "After a night of agony, she would emerge from her struggle with a radiant face and luminous eyes, and they would hesitate to speak to her for fear of disturbing the peace which enveloped her." But before long she was writing energetically to a student in Boston: "Hold the fort for I am coming. . . . I hope my forty days in the wilderness are about over." And after a few weeks back in Boston she wrote another student: "The ship of Science is again mounting the waves, rising above the billows, bidding defiance to the floodgates of error, for God is at the helm." [18]

Her growing emphasis on the positive is well illustrated by a change made in one of her successive revisions of *Science and Health*. In the first edition she had written: "Evil thoughts reach farther, and do more harm than individual crimes. . . . When malicious purposes, evil thoughts, or lusts, go forth from one mind, they seek others and will lodge in them unless repelled by virtue and a higher motive for being." In a later edition this becomes: "Evil thoughts and aims reach no farther and do no more harm than one's belief permits. Evil thoughts, lusts, and malicious purposes cannot go forth, like wandering pollen, from one human mind to another, finding unsuspected lodgment, if virtue and truth build a strong defence." The doctrine is the same, but the emphasis entirely different. The accent is on victory.

---

[18] Longyear, *The Genealogy and Life of Asa Gilbert Eddy*, pp. 77 ff.

From now on students flocked to her from all parts of the country, while Boston began to sit up and take notice. She had already moved her headquarters from provincial Lynn to "the Hub." In 1881 she had founded her Massachusetts Metaphysical College, and among the several clergymen listed on the Board of Visitors was William R. Alger, Theodore Parker's successor in the pastorate of the Society of Liberal Christians and a lecturer at the Concord School of Philosophy. Cyrus Bartol, who had never ceased to be a Transcendentalist since the formation of the Transcendental Club in 1836, listened to Mrs. Eddy's explanations and declared: "I have preached the living God for forty years, but never felt His presence and power as you do," and delivered two sermons from his pulpit in her defense.[19]

Edward Everett Hale, at that time the most popular minister in Boston, wrote of her: "She has taught me more truth in twenty minutes than I have learned in twenty years," and Wendell Phillips, perhaps the noblest of the Abolitionists and always a passionate champion of freedom, was reported to have said: "Had I young blood in my veins, I would help that woman."

Even conservative Cambridge stepped forward to support her, in the person of Andrew P. Peabody, Plummer Professor of Christian Morals and Preacher to Harvard University, Emeritus, a man held in affection and esteem by three generations of Harvard men. When Christian Science was under particularly heavy assault from the Boston pulpits in 1884, Dr. Peabody preached for her congregation on five different occasions. And other younger clergymen, like O. P. Gifford of the Warren Avenue Baptist Church, studied with her and became defenders of her teachings without ever actually becoming Christian Scientists.

---

[19] See *The Cross and the Crown* by Norman Beasley (New York and Boston, Duell, Sloan, and Pearce–Little, Brown and Co., 1952), p. 124.

Nevertheless, the attacks were still far heavier than the support she received. The Reverend Joseph Cook, friend and admirer of Bronson Alcott and conductor of the immensely popular though intellectually pretentious Monday Lectures at Tremont Temple, lent his platform to a violent attack on Mrs. Eddy by the Reverend A. J. Gordon; and when she was grudgingly granted ten minutes to make a reply on a subsequent Monday morning, it was Cook who frigidly introduced her with the words, "It becomes my interesting duty to introduce to this audience, Mrs. Eddy." That was typical of the suspicion and cold hostility which she met even from some who had a good deal of sympathy with earlier Transcendental aims.

To their eyes she seemed only one more of the innumerable cranks and fakirs of the Boston of that period. Failing to recognize the magnitude and uniqueness of what she was saying, they failed to differentiate her from the assorted charlatans who cluttered the scene. This was the society acidly drawn by Henry James in *The Bostonians,* with its "great irregular army of nostrum-mongers, domiciled in humanitary Bohemia," its intellectually shoddy campfollowers like Mrs. Tarrant, who "had partaken of the comfort of a hundred religions, had followed innumerable dietary reforms, chiefly of the negative order, and had gone of an evening to a *séance* or a lecture as regularly as she had eaten her supper." All this peeping and muttering, this mind-curing and spirit-rapping, seemed a far less healthy thing than the efflorescence of youthful vitality that was evident in the days of the Chardon Street convention forty years before, and it was and is hard for many critics to credit the possibility that a new movement radiant with spiritual health should emerge in such a faded milieu. On the other hand, it has been pointed out that to the ancient Roman, critical of the restless and jaded tastes of his fellow citizens, Christianity itself at first seemed to be only one more of the fashionable mystery cults imported from the East.

Another aspect of the scene that incensed many a beholder was what Basil Ransom of *The Bostonians* called its "damnable feminisation." The genteel female of the period had turned subversive; she appeared on the one hand to be covertly imposing on society the standards of false gentility which, in the first place, it had imposed on *her*, and on the other hand to be overtly breaking out in a graceless feminism which brazenly challenged the male on his own ground. James's Basil Ransom spoke for many when he declared:

> I am so far from thinking . . . that there is not enough woman in our general life, that it has long been pressed home to me that there is a great deal too much. The whole generation is womanised; the masculine tone is passing out of the world; it's a feminine, a nervous, hysterical, chattering, canting age, an age of hollow phrases and false delicacy and exaggerated solicitudes and coddled sensibilities, which, if we don't soon look out, will usher in the reign of mediocrity, of the feeblest and flattest and the most pretentious that has ever been. The masculine character, and ability to dare and endure, to know and yet not fear reality, to look the world in the face and take it for what it is—a very queer and partly very base mixture—that is what I want to preserve, or rather, as I may say, to recover. . . .

It is against this background that one must see much of the misunderstanding and obloquy that greeted Mrs. Eddy at this time.[20] Though Alcott in his first letter to her in regard to *Science and Health* had been able to rejoice that "the blessed words are of woman's divinings," and though other liberal souls might be able to grant the possibility that a pure, forward thrust of spirit should come through wom-

---

[20] See Mary Burt Messer, *The Family in the Making* (New York, G. P. Putnam's Sons, 1928), Chap. XXIV, for an acute appraisal of Christian Science in relation to the rise of feminism.

an's insight, it was all too easy to lose the distinctive metaphysical tone of her teachings in the trivial hubbub around her. The newspapers were beginning to refer to her glibly as the "Boston Prophetess," and Professor L. T. Townsend of Boston University christened her teachings the "Boston Craze." In a widely quoted lecture on the subject in 1884 he burst out: "This woman claims to be the originator of a new system of philosophy and healing. Were there consistency enough in her teachings to constitute a philosophy it would be called a crude attempt to resuscitate the defunct idealism of the nihilistic type which appeared in the middle ages. Her views upon metaphysical matters—we speak very mildly—are a self-contradictory hotch-potch." [21]

Part of the trouble was that people were always confusing Mrs. Eddy's system with the innumerable varieties of "mind-cure" which were springing up around it, devoid of its rational basis or spiritual altitude but aping its methods, borrowing its terminology and even its name. This was pointed up by a letter from Louisa M. Alcott published in the *Woman's Journal* in April, 1885. Bronson's famous daughter had worn herself out earning a living for the family which her father's improvidence had virtually left to the charity of the elements. Deeply devoted to Alcott though she was, she had learned to be deeply skeptical of his Transcendental enthusiasms, and only dire need finally induced her to turn to what she called "the mind-cure."

It seems likely that early in 1885 she actually paid Mrs. Eddy a visit. Many years later her friend Katherine Conway of *The Pilot* told Sibyl Wilbur: "Miss Alcott, though her fa-

---

[21] Cf. the conclusion of Henry W. Steiger in *Christian Science and Philosophy* that Christian Science is "a coherent whole, a self-sufficient system of thought," as well as a successful practice. Interestingly enough, this careful academic study was done in 1945-46 as a doctoral dissertation, under the guidance of Edgar S. Brightman, in the philosophy department of Boston University, from which Townsend's blast had issued sixty-odd years before.

ther was a transcendentalist and some years before had more than half avowed a faith in the new system of metaphysics, did not take to it. She was of a very practical, matter-of-fact mind. She had had enough of idealism and was determined to keep her feet upon terra firma. But she was impressed with Mrs. Eddy's personality." There is some doubt about this incident, for Miss Conway also claimed that Louisa Alcott was accompanied on her visit by Frances Hodgson Burnett, whereas the latter's son, himself a Christian Scientist, has authoritatively denied that his mother ever met Mrs. Eddy. This throws some uncertainty on the whole story, but it is unimportant in any case. For when Louisa, in desperate mood, decided to have treatment for "writer's cramp and an overworked brain," she turned to a healer who called herself a Christian Scientist but had no connection whatever with Mrs. Eddy or her teachings.

The treatment was unsuccessful, she explained in her letter to the *Woman's Journal,* and no effect was felt "except sleepiness for the first few times; then mesmeric suggestions occasionally came, sunshine in the head, a sense of walking on the air, and slight trances, when it was impossible to stir for a few moments." So she returned to the "homeopathy and massage" from which she had been lured by the hope of a quick cure—and, it must be regretfully recorded, to the early grave which awaited her four years later.

The letter caused a considerable stir. Here was an example of the popular misunderstanding that Mrs. Eddy faced in presenting her Science to the world. It was obvious from the effects described by Miss Alcott that the "treatment" she received was no more Christian Science than it was astronomy or physics, yet in the public mind the two were lumped together as variants of a single practice. Mrs. Eddy was frequently referred to in the press as a mind-curist, while Miss Alcott's would-be healer and others like her did not hesitate to call themselves Christian Scientists. However, the incident provided an opportunity to write letters of explanation to the press, drawing the line of distinction more clearly. One statement which received wide circulation was from Mrs. Eddy's secretary, Calvin Frye, and read in part: "That those acquainted with the facts may not misapprehend the method used in [Miss Alcott's] case, it seems proper to state authoritatively that 'mind cure' is not Christian Science, and no member of the Christian Scientists' Association, Church, or College, conducted her case. The 'sensations' of which she speaks, are at variance with the teachings and practice of Christian Science." It was clear, Frye concluded, that Miss Alcott was a victim of the "mental malpractice" or mesmerism so often denounced by Mrs. Eddy.

Nothing has met with more resistance from critics of Christian Science than Mrs. Eddy's assertion that, whereas her system of healing rested on a genuinely metaphysical or scientifically spiritual basis, all other forms of mental healing were to be ascribed to the "human mind," to mental suggestion, will power, blind faith, or personal magnetism, rather than to the divine Mind. Her claim was bound up, as we have seen, with a radical metaphysical position. However cloudy the propositions of Christian Science may look to a critical outsider, to the serious Christian Scientist they seem to have a sort of mathematical purity, a structural precision which admits of no slightest deviation.

The Christian Scientist is constantly on the alert in his mental practice to reject the arguments of "personal sense" which would substitute his will for God's, his wisdom for the divine purposes, his humanly mental effort for the divine Mind's energies. Through experience he finds the basic terminology worked out by Mrs. Eddy over many years to be essential to his preserving that razor-edged accuracy of spiritual sensibility that will allow him to discriminate between the suggestions of mortal mind and the impartations of the divine Mind.

If this seems to indicate an illiberal attitude on his part toward the conscientious people who may practice "mental healing" in one form or another, it can only be answered that the Christian Scientist's quarrel is never with persons, as Mrs. Eddy pointed out more and more clearly as she went on. In *Science and Health* she wrote: "Those individuals who adopt theosophy, spiritualism, or hypnotism, may possess natures above some others who eschew their false beliefs. Therefore my contest is not with the individual, but with the false system." And again she wrote: "A genuine Christian Scientist loves Protestant and Catholic, D.D. and M.D.,—loves all who love God, good; and he loves his enemies." Of the much-misunderstood "malicious animal magnetism," she wrote in 1889 that the hour had passed for it to be treated personally, and that it must now be dealt with as impersonal evil, not as an evildoer, and thus be reduced to its ultimate status as false claim or nothingness. But she never ceased to insist that any form of mental practice which departed from her fundamental metaphysical position was dangerous because it failed to deny the "old man" whom St. Paul had declared must be put off in order that the "new man" after Christ might appear.

Among the welter of "mind-curists" at that time, some of them disaffected students of hers who found her leadership too exacting and her doctrine too rigorous, the one common denominator seemed to be some sense of the "God within" or the "Christ within." Yet without the denial of corporeal personality and its own will to control, Mrs. Eddy felt there was mortal danger of identifying God with one's unregenerate human inclinations. She felt that her own acute awareness of this danger, as well as the continual inspiration welling up from her initial discovery of the allness of Spirit, fitted her uniquely for the leadership of the new movement. But some who responded eagerly to the inspiration had little taste for the denials which accompanied it in her case.

Take Lilian Whiting, for instance—the impressionable young journalist who had written so lyrically of the Concord School of Philosophy. A month or two after Louisa Alcott's letter in the *Woman's Journal,* Miss Whiting interviewed Mrs. Eddy. She had had no previous contact with either Mrs. Eddy or any of her students and knew little or nothing about Christian Science and the mind-cure movement. She went, she declared, with no particular feeling of either skepticism or expectation, but simply as a journalist on assignment. In the published interview which appeared in the *Ohio Leader,* she told of the favorable impression made on her by Mrs. Eddy's "cordial and graceful" manner, but the most striking part of the published interview was its final paragraph:

> Mrs. Eddy impressed me as a woman who is—in the language of our Methodist friends—"filled with the spirit." It seems to be a merely natural gift with her. She is, by nature, a harmonizer. My own personal experience in that call was so singular that I will venture to relate it. I went, as I have already said, in a journalistic spirit. I had no belief, or disbelief, and the idea of getting any personal benefit from the call, save matter for press use, never occurred to me. But I remembered afterward how extremely tired I was as I walked rather wearily and languidly up the steps to Mrs. Eddy's door. I came away, as a little child friend of mine expressively says, "skipping." I was at least a mile from the Vendome, and I walked home feeling as if I were treading on air. My sleep that night was the rest of elysium. If I had been caught up into paradise it could hardly have been a more wonderful renewal. All the next day this exalted state continued. I can hardly describe it; it was simply the most marvelous elasticity of mind and body. All this time—it was Saturday evening I called on Mrs. Eddy, and the ensuing day being Sunday, and not attending service

that day, I was not out to meet anyone—all this Sunday I merely thought a trifle wonderingly, "How well I feel." In the evening I had callers, and I told of my visit to Mrs. Eddy, and later, in an entirely different connection, I chanced to allude to the unusual, and indeed, utterly unprecedented buoyancy and energy I was feeling. "Why that's the result of your going to Mrs. Eddy," explained a friend who had heard of her powers. I had not thought of it before, because you see I went to have my mind stored, not cured, and, in the journalistic sense, I forgot I was with the most famous "mind-curer" of the day. Whether my half hour's talk with her produced this result I do not know. At least, here are the facts.

One might assume from this that Miss Whiting would be attracted to Christian Science. She did in fact visit Mrs. Eddy several times again and remained admiring and friendly until the latter's retirement from Boston; but like so many others on whom the Christian Science leader made an immensely favorable impression she was drawn by temperament to the more congenial group of assorted Mental Scientists, disaffected Christian Scientists, Faith Healers and others who formed the Church of the Divine Unity. In this hospitable atmosphere was to be found that exuberant open-mindedness which welcomed any and all manifestations of the Spirit, or even of the spirits. Cyrus Bartol was inevitably drawn here, and other ministers who had been introduced to the subject of spiritual healing by Mrs. Eddy likewise gravitated toward a religious society where each could follow his vagrant inspiration without reference to a sharply defined and demanding metaphysic.

From this group and others like it the New Thought movement developed. It is no part of the purpose of this book to criticize one movement from the point of view of another, but simply to draw necessary lines of distinction. To the advocate of New Thought, Christian Science appeared narrow and dogmatic, especially in its insistence on the absolute unreality of matter. To the Christian Scientist, on the other hand, the "way" of scientific Christian metaphysics must necessarily be as strait and narrow as the discipline of physics, in which subjective preference is not to be substituted for objective fact. Understandably but regrettably the outsider looking in on both movements has usually failed to recognize the enormous differences which separate the one from the other.

The eclecticism of New Thought was evident in the various sources on which it drew. One of these was the "New Church" of Emanuel Swedenborg. Warren F. Evans, a Swedenborgian clergyman who had closely observed the healings of P. P. Quimby and who became one of the early leaders in the mental-healing movement, reflected Swedenborg's conviction that the cause of disease is spiritual evil.

The movement owed a conscious and more important debt to Emerson, who was "discovered" in this connection by Charles M. Barrows in 1887. The Emersonian doctrine that "the soul makes circumstance" was admirably adapted to a point of view which found typical expression in the formula presented by Henry Wood, one of the most popular New Thought writers, for frequent repetition:

> I am soul and spirit.
> I am at one with the Universal Good.
> Harmony, love, strength and wholeness are with and in me.
> I rule the body and delight in it as a holy temple.
> I rightfully claim the control of all my powers, mental and physical.

It is necessary to insist again how far removed from Christian Science this is, not merely in doctrine but in *atmosphere*. For one thing, Mrs. Eddy forbade the repetition of verbal formulas. For another, Soul and Spirit were synonyms for

God, not to be claimed by the human consciousness, which must learn to say with Jesus: "I can of mine own self do nothing. . . . The Father that dwelleth in me, he doeth the works. . . . Why callest thou me good? there is none good but one, that is, God." To the Christian Scientist, as to the traditional Christian, the danger of spiritual presumptuousness in such affirmations as Henry Wood's seems very real.

New Thought is an important link between one aspect of Transcendental thinking and the popular success-psychology of present-day America. It is in the direct line between Emerson's statement, "Shun the negative side. Never wrong people with your contritions, nor with dismal views of politics or society. Never name sickness . . ." and modern inspirational works on the power of positive thinking. The historian of New Thought, Horatio W. Dresser, writes characteristically of the movement: "It has fostered the type of optimism for which America stands. It has helped in productive enterprises, in stimulating the constructive attitude. Its influence is seen in what may be called 'the psychology of success,' wherever the value of expectant suggestion is seen."

We are back at the word "suggestion," so totally unacceptable in Christian Science. Only as one recognizes Mrs. Eddy's constant, unremitting efforts to set a metaphysical line of demarcation between spiritual understanding and mental suggestion can one comprehend what New Thought writers have called her authoritarianism or narrow exclusiveness.

"She is a woman of one idea almost to wearisomeness," wrote Thomas Van Ness, a young Unitarian minister who came all the way from Denver especially to investigate her teachings. To him it was a disappointment to find that she was not interested in identifying herself with the larger light of idealism that haloed New England thought. Many years later he wrote: "I asked Mrs. Eddy one afternoon, when we were talking on the subject of her plans, whether she cared much for the teachings of Emerson, to me the noblest of New England's inspirers. Her reply was vague, the subject did not interest her and we soon drifted away from it. . . ." [22]

Van Ness, who never grasped the revolutionary logic of her position, was baffled by what he considered her "double nature"—her intuitive spirituality on the one hand, and on the other her insistence on discipline and her denunciation of the malice of mortal mind. "She has abundant determination," he wrote in his diary at the time. "She wants absolute obedience. I can imagine if I accepted her offer to come on to Boston and lecture at Chickering Hall, I would have to be her slave; yet there is a sweetness about the woman, too. . . ." [23]

Another Unitarian minister (or rather, ex-minister) with an ambivalent attitude toward the Christian Science leader was the cultivated Bostonian, James Henry Wiggin, who became her literary adviser in the middle eighties. To many of his friends he expressed considerable admiration for this remarkable woman, yet at times his intellectual vanity rebelled at her approach to metaphysics through experience rather than through the formal rigors of philosophy and theology, at what seemed to his ponderously masculine judgment her feminine irrationalities—and at her unwillingness

---

[22] Thomas Van Ness, *The Religion of New England* (Boston, Beacon Press, 1926), pp. 166 ff.

[23] *Ibid.* The last phrase falls into a pattern that recurs frequently in comments by those who met Mrs. Eddy. Cf. Alcott's statement (p. 87): "There is perhaps a touch of fanaticism, *though of a genial quality*, interposed into her faith. . . ." Cf. also the statement of Allan McLane Hamilton, the distinguished psychiatrist who examined her to test her mental competency at the time of the Next Friends' Suit in 1907: "In her ordinary conversation she is witty, a bit satirical, *but with a great deal of gentleness in her demeanor*. . . ." (New York *Times*, August 25, 1907. Italics added.)

to adopt many of his suggestions for "improving" her manuscript.

He succeeded in persuading her to introduce into the sixteenth edition of *Science and Health* a number of quotations from various Transcendental writers and even from the Bhagavad-Gita, but she later removed them from the book, thus bearing out her own statement made in 1906: "In almost every case where Mr. Wiggin added words, I have erased them in my revisions." Today many of the quotations which he labored to introduce into the book have a curiously dated air, and Mrs. Eddy's removal of them is a tribute to her sounder instinct for the final integrity of her work.

Wiggin himself, early in his association with her, under the pseudonym of Phare Pleigh wrote a pamphlet in defense of Christian Science in which he paid tribute to her character:

> Whatever is to be Mrs. Eddy's future reputation, time will show. Little cares she, if only through her work the Truth may be glorified. More than once, in her earnestness, she has reached her bottom dollar, but the interest of the world to hear her word has always filled her coffers anew. Within a few months she has made sacrifices, from which most authors would have shrunk, to ensure the moral rightness of her book. This statement Phare Pleigh makes out of his own personal and peculiar knowledge of the circumstances. Day after day flew by, and weeks lengthened into months; from every quarter came importunate missives of inquiry and mercantile reproach; hundreds of dollars were sunk in a bottomless sea of corrections; yet not till the authoress was satisfied that her duty was wholly done, would she allow printer and binder to send forth her book to the world.

Again he wrote:

> In her simple way of trying to get at the centre of Christian Truth, Mrs. Eddy proves herself no mean expositor of Scrip-

ture, and often grasps, unaided, certain facts,—about the Books of the Bible, for instance,—which are in accord with the most advanced scholarship: though she has not reached her knowledge through scholastic instruction, and has been rather surprised when the confirmatory literary facts have afterwards come within her ken. . . .

These statements contrast strikingly with the contemptuously cynical picture of her which he is reported to have drawn for two critical friends in later years. Even before his relationship with Mrs. Eddy terminated, she complained on one occasion of the "shocking flippancy" of some of his comments on the proof sheets he returned to her. It seems probable that his essentially worldly nature ended by reacting sharply from this incomprehensibly self-assured woman to whom he felt so intellectually superior—and perhaps, in a disturbing way, so spiritually inferior. Yet Mrs. Eddy always wrote of him afterward with gratitude and admiration, and it may well be that the later views attributed to him grossly misrepresent his deepest feelings about *Science and Health* and its author.[24]

In the same year in which Wiggin first met Mrs. Eddy, a particularly sweeping attack on Christian Science by the Reverend Stacy Fowler was published in the *Homiletic Review*. Fowler extended his criticism of Mrs. Eddy's personal leadership to her whole doctrine of personality:

---

[24] The more extended criticism he is supposed to have made occurred in an article published in 1906. This article purported to set forth what Wiggin had told a friend about Mrs. Eddy seven years earlier, a few months before his death. Critics have repeatedly quoted from this article as though it were a *letter* written by Wiggin to his friend. One recent critic even states categorically that this criticism was "from the pen of the Rev. J. H. Wiggin himself." A careful reading of the article shows that not one word in it was written by Wiggin. From beginning to end it merely records what the author—who makes no attempt to conceal his corrosive animosity toward Mrs. Eddy—says that Wiggin told him years before.

Ostensibly the "Science" rests on a theological basis. It starts with a peculiar idea of God as an impersonal being. But if man is not a *person* there is no ground for a reasonable psychology. You cannot construct a science of soul if the soul has no personal identity, no real *ego* of its own. Thought thus becomes too vague and diffused to be brought into order and sequence. Of course if there is no basis for reasonable psychology, then there can be none for reasonable theology, philosophy, or science. Deny human personality and you are floating in thin ether. All sound reasoning begins with the conscious human ego. I think, I am; and the I am of thought is conscious personality. You might as well attempt to rise to the stars by holding to the string of a kite, as to attempt to project yourself into God by denying your own personalism. . . .

Here is the second great theoretical problem Christian Science confronts with a unique answer, the first being the philosophical question as to the origin of so-called mortal mind. And again its answer is a practical one, making the objection part of the very misconception that is wiped out by the practical "demonstration."

Alcott, at his last visit to Mrs. Eddy, had recognized "the faith with which she ventures into hitherto unexplored crypts of psychology," even though he denied her an "established philosophy." The most hard-bitten critic would have to grant her at least an empirical skill in psychology; the very magnitude of her practical achievements bears witness to that. Her official title, Discoverer and Founder of Christian Science, recognizes that she "discovered" a system and "founded" an institution; it pays tribute to a theory and a practice, a religion and a church, a philosophy and a psychology.

She herself wrote of "the deep demand for the Science of psychology." But she spelled the word science in this connection with a capital S; her statement signified no moving toward the currents of academic, clinical, or popular psychology, as New Thought was to do in its later phases. The psychologist and psychiatrist, like the physician and physicist, must move over in her direction if there was ever to be a real *rapprochement*.

Her psychology starts with the experience of a "new birth" in individual human consciousness. This consciousness was not to be confused with mortal mind. The human mind was that point in conscious experience in which good and evil, Truth and error, the illuminations of the divine Mind and the suggestions of mortal mind, seemed to meet, mingle, and do battle. In some persons the good might seem very feeble, in others superbly strong and active; yet in either case it appeared to be an inextricable part of a human personality, apparently determined by heredity, environment, education, and the million complex influences of a material creation. No matter how effective the good in a particular individual might be, mortal mind (acting through personal sense) claimed to put limits to it, to couple it with undesirable characteristics, to weaken or pervert it with the inescapable frailties and fallibilities of human nature. Even the concept of good differed endlessly from person to person, and in all the rich confusion of human personality there was no point of absolute rest or certainty. To reach that point one must start with Jesus' uncompromising statement, "Ye must be born again."

To be born again was to discover one's pre-existent spiritual identity, fashioned wholly by Spirit and not by material history. It was to come to oneself, to awake to that higher selfhood made in the image and likeness of God, of infinite good, admitting no contradictions or limitations, no corruptions or diminutions. It was to identify oneself as idea, not matter; as individualized expression of Soul, of the one, infinite, divine Person, not as fallen soul or finite personality, subject to all the vagaries of the mortal sense of life.

There are several things that this did *not* mean. It did not mean that Christian Science was Vedanta or any of those forms of Hindu and Buddhist teaching to which New Thought, in some of its phases, inclined. Christian Science did not teach the absorption of the individual in God, or the annihilation of identity within the divine Mind. Each idea of Mind, each reflection of Soul, was eternally distinct, an imperishable part of the infinitely varied expression of the creative Principle, Love. Mrs. Eddy explicitly wrote: "This scientific sense of being, forsaking matter for Spirit, by no means suggests man's absorption into Deity and the loss of his identity, but confers upon man enlarged individuality, a wider sphere of thought and action, a more expansive love, a higher and more permanent peace." Such a sense inevitably included a clearer perception of the true identity of one's fellow man, and an increasing recognition of the pre-existent harmony of all the sons, or ideas, of God.

Nor was this to be considered pantheism, in any generally recognized sense of the word. Mrs. Eddy's language might sometimes sound pantheistic, but not her thought. In fact, her complaint was that all the common systems of thought were pantheistic. If God was Life, then to believe that life was in molecular structures was pantheism. If God was Mind, to believe that intelligence was in brain cells was pantheism. God, Soul, was not even *in* His spiritual manifestation, any more than the sun was in its rays. Instead, His manifestation—the ideal man, including all right ideas—existed in Him as the object of His thought, the witness of His nature.

God was conscious and infinite Person, for Mrs. Eddy's use of the word Principle for Deity did not imply a lifeless, abstract, unconscious *thing*.[25] Rather, it defined divine Love, the synonym she so often coupled with Principle, as that which tenderly, undeviatingly held each individual manifestation of its nature in ordered, harmonious, law-abiding relation with all the rest. Thus when she repeatedly ranged Principle against personality, it was the Principle of each individual's divine identity against the finite, mortal personality which argues so hard for its own view of things.

The psychology of Christian Science—or its "anatomy," to use the word she sometimes employed in a way reminiscent of Robert Burton—consisted in the dissection of individual consciousness to discover whether the thoughts presenting themselves for acceptance proceeded from the divine Mind or its supposititious opposite. This meant a constant process of separating between one's true identity and the false characteristics and limitations that would try to attach themselves to this identity (like "wagon-loads of offal"), claiming origin in an inescapable material past.

In actual daily life one must talk pragmatically of this individual human consciousness, this subjective arena of moral struggle, as "I," even as Jesus did when he said "Not as I will, but as thou wilt." But speaking as the Christ, the wholly spiritual manifestation of God, the Saviour had said, "I and my Father are one," and as the Christ dawned in each individual human consciousness, unfolding one's true identity as individualized expression of the divine Ego or I Am, it began at once to dissipate the false beliefs that clamored, "I am sick," "I am frightened," "I am angry, frustrated, complacent, greedy, decrepit, self-willed, confused, enslaved, in despair." The human consciousness was grad-

---

[25] In an interesting comparison between Christian Science and philosophical Personalism, Steiger (*Christian Science and Philosophy*, p. 137) contrasts both with "the pantheistic view of the universe as composed of particles of spiritual energy—spiritual objects without a unifying subject."

ually transformed, like a darkened room in which the shutters are little by little opened until the room is flooded with light.[26]

Human consciousness, then, was a transitional state of "becoming," and the progressive appearing of the divine in it brought out all those transitional qualities that are rightly called *humane*—the courage and compassion and patience which reach out to a sick, scared, hungry world with the promise of something better. "The divinity of the Christ," wrote Mrs. Eddy in a memorable sentence, "was made manifest in the humanity of Jesus." And it might be said that the radical metaphysic of Christian Science was made manifest in the humane psychology of its application to human needs.

Nowhere is this more apparent than in the successive revisions of *Science and Health,* each one designed to reach more effectively the different states and stages of thought she was addressing. Occasional students of Christian Science have said they preferred the starker statements of the first edition to the more gracious approach of the last; but if so, they show that they know little about human nature, little about the necessary preparation of the human mind to receive those deep flashes of revelation which dispossess it of any claim to entity apart from God. It might be added parenthetically that most of the "contradictions" which critics delight in pointing out in the book disappear as soon as one understands that she is speaking now in the "absolute," now in the "relative," at one moment addressing that consciousness of divine being which constitutes man's spiritual selfhood, at the next addressing the limited human consciousness of good on which the new sense of being is dawn-

---

26 See Mrs. Eddy's article on "The New Birth" in her *Miscellaneous Writings,* especially her statement: "The new birth is not the work of a moment. It begins with moments, and goes on with years; moments of surrender to God, of childlike trust and joyful adoption of good; moments of self-abnegation, self-consecration, heaven-born hope, and spiritual love."

ing, or again addressing that darkened state of human thought which nevertheless may cry out honestly with the publican commended by Jesus, "God be merciful to me a sinner."

Nothing is more instructive in this respect than to note the changes which Christian Science wrought in Mrs. Eddy herself. Both friends and foes have often erred in failing to recognize the transformation of her personality which took place under the influence of the tremendous idea that broke on her, supplemented by the often bitter experience through which she passed in giving that idea to the world. They have frequently assumed that the Mrs. Eddy of 1866 was exactly the same Mrs. Eddy who greeted Alcott in 1876, and that the vigorous crusader of the eighties did not differ in any important respect from the world-renowned figure who in 1901 and again in 1902 declared: "Follow your Leader, only so far as she follows Christ," and who wrote in the preface to the final edition of *Science and Health:* "To-day, though rejoicing in some progress, she [the author] still finds herself a willing disciple at the heavenly gate, waiting for the Mind of Christ."

What remained constant was the *idea,* and this idea included the pre-existent spiritual perfection of every child of God—including, of course, Mrs. Eddy herself. But as various sympathetic observers have noted, time and experience were required to bring out the conservatism and restraint which marked her later years, the mellow "humanistic" qualities to which such a Boston Brahmin as William Dana Orcutt has borne witness, the patience that could wait for years until her followers were ready to take a necessary forward step, the charity that could refrain even from self-defense when to answer would be to expose another's weakness.[27]

---

[27] See Powell, *Mary Baker Eddy: A Life Size Portrait,* p. 214 f., for an account of her refusal to vindicate herself in a difficult situation by permit-

In nothing, perhaps, was her greatness more clearly shown than in her extraordinary capacity for growth.

Mrs. Eddy herself never claimed to be humanly perfect. Jesus of Nazareth, she declared, was the "only immaculate." He was the perfect Exemplar, and never did she claim human equality with him, though she did claim divine equality for all the sons of God in their spiritual status as "joint heirs with Christ." What Jesus was by virtue of his "original scientific sonship with God," others must become through the "supremely natural transforming power of Truth"—and in this respect she placed herself with the Apostle Paul, whose work she once spoke of carrying on to its logical conclusion.[28]

In her autobiography, *Retrospection and Introspection,* she put the matter clearly:

> Jesus of Nazareth was a natural and divine Scientist. He was so before the material world saw him. He who antedated Abraham, and gave the world a new date in the Christian era, was a Christian Scientist, who needed no discovery of the Science of being in order to rebuke the evidence. To one "born of the flesh," however, divine Science must be a discovery.

Here she speaks of herself plainly as one "born of the flesh" and thereby requiring the new birth which the Founder of Christianity did not need because his unique birth had endowed him from the outset with the pure Christ-nature. Though insistent on the importance of recognizing her place as Discoverer and Founder of Christian Science, and supremely assured that God had called her to the leadership of the Christian Science movement, she expressed always the deepest love and reverence for the Master whose

---

ting the publication of the thoroughly persuasive documentary study, *Mrs. Eddy and the Late Suit in Equity,* by Michael Meehan. See also correspondence in *The Lutheran Quarterly,* vol. VII, no. 1 (February, 1955), pp. 69–76.

[28] *Miscellaneous Writings,* p. 188.

latter-day disciple she felt herself to be. But she looked at him with fresh eyes, as though the Councils of Nicaea and Chalcedon and all the centuries-old encrustations of doctrine had never been.

It has sometimes been suggested that her teaching of the unreality of matter denied the incarnation and that her conviction that evil and suffering are delusions of mortal sense robbed the crucifixion and resurrection of all meaning. This is to take her teachings in a most superficial way. Innumerable passages in her writings, of which the two following are typical, point to the reverse:

> Born of a woman, Jesus' advent in the flesh partook partly of Mary's earthly condition, although he was endowed with the Christ, the divine Spirit, without measure. This accounts for his struggles in Gethsemane and on Calvary, and this enabled him to be the mediator, or *way-shower,* between God and men. Had his origin and birth been wholly apart from mortal usage, Jesus would not have been appreciable to mortal mind as "the way."

> While we adore Jesus, and the heart overflows with gratitude for what he did for mortals,—treading alone his loving pathway up to the throne of glory, in speechless agony exploring the way for us,—yet Jesus spares us not one individual experience, if we follow his commands faithfully; and all have the cup of sorrowful effort to drink in proportion to their demonstration of his love, till all are redeemed through divine Love.

Here is the deeper note which sounds again and again beneath the triumphant affirmations of Christian Science. Mrs. Eddy very purposefully chose the cross and the crown—crucifixion and resurrection, trial and victory—as the symbol of Christian Science. This was the point that William James was to miss in *The Varieties of Religious Experience* when he lumped Christian Science and New Thought together indiscriminately as optimistic religions of the "once-born."

Because Christian Science shared the radiant New Testament sense of the triumph of the resurrection, because it said with Jesus, "If a man keep my saying, he shall never see death," and with Paul, "I can do all things through Christ which strengtheneth me," it was easy for an outsider to see it as only another form of cheerful healthy-mindedness.

Significantly enough, Mrs. Eddy uses the word "optimism" only once in all her writings, and then in a most unexpected way. It occurs in a passage which sums up effectively the relative psychology of Christian Science as distinct from its absolute metaphysics:

> The nature of the individual, more stubborn than the circumstance, will always be found arguing for itself,—its habits, tastes, and indulgences. This material nature strives to tip the beam against the spiritual nature; for the flesh strives against Spirit,—against whatever or whoever opposes evil,—and weighs mightily in the scale against man's high destiny. This conclusion is not an argument either for pessimism or for optimism, but is a plea for free moral agency,—full exemption from all necessity to obey a power that should be and is found powerless in Christian Science.

In the light of the foregoing discussion, it is interesting to turn back to what Paul Elmer More calls the "jaunty optimism" of Emerson. More, who blandly characterizes Christian Science as "a diluted and stale product of Emersonianism," goes on to say:

> There is a story—how authentic I do not know—that when Emerson was visiting Carlyle, the gruff Scotchman, who certainly believed heartily in evil and damnation, carried his guest to the slums of London and pointed out to him one horrible sight after another. "And do you believe in the deil, noo?" he would say; and always Emerson would shake his head in gentle denial. The story is at least *ben trovato;* it sets forth clearly the facile optimism out of which Christian Science was

to spring. Such a creed, when professed by one who spoke with the noble accent and from the deep insight of an Emerson, was a radiant possession for seeking humanity forever; it is folly and inner deception when repeated parrot-like by men and women with no mental training and, visibly to all the world, with no warrant of spiritual experience.[29]

The urbane snobbery of such a passage, with its total unawareness of the dynamics of Christian Science healing, makes one wonder whether More, the Christian, would have turned in distaste from the untrained minds and spontaneous enthusiasm of the small group of commonplace people who took to the ancient world the improbable gospel, "Christ is risen!"

There was something of the atmosphere of primitive Christianity among the little group of faithful who surrounded Mrs. Eddy in the eighties; there was storm and struggle and persecution, but also a sense of boundless possibilities, the shining assurance of the new-born of Spirit. William Lyman Johnson, who participated as a boy in the activities of those days, compares the atmosphere to that of Brook Farm; but these were simpler, less intellectual people, though touched by the fire of a great vision. In a charming little reminiscence, naïve and nostalgic, Johnson describes their suppers at a small restaurant on Tremont Street before the Friday evening meetings of those days:

This old-fashioned type restaurant, which ran through to Tamworth Street, was long and narrow, always well-lighted, and always neat. It had about it an air of comfort, and here came Miss Bartlett, Mr. and Mrs. Munroe, Mrs. Colman, Mrs. Williams, Mr. and Mrs. Landy, Captain and Mrs. Eastaman, Mr. Mason, Mr. Bailey, father, mother, and myself. Miss Bartlett and the Munroes usually made up a table with us, and

---

[29] *Shelburne Essays*, First Series (Boston, Houghton Mifflin, 1904), p. 80 f.

sometimes Mr. Mason would join in pleasant comradeship. Here, over a simple meal, the work that was laid out for the coming week and the experiences of each since they had last met would be talked over. A review of what the Teacher had said to them at the College would follow, or the result of a meeting held for some special purpose; then questions on the interpretation of passages of Scripture and of *Science and Health*. This hour of the evening meal was filled with a wonderful sweetness. There was a free and generous exchange of thought, a simple association which bore the fruits of faithfulness and unity, while there was always a pervading perfume, since some one had seen Mrs. Eddy yesterday or today, and the few words which she had spoken opened new vistas of the truth that they must seek for and find.

There was no idolatry among these early Scientists. They were not sentimentalists for they had been tried in the fires of struggle and the battles for right. They were middle-aged people who had learned much of the world before coming into Science, and the quiet and reverent way in which they referred to the Teacher, their gentleness, and their ever-present love, spoke the impress which the spirit of Mrs. Eddy had made, a spirit that was ever with us at our meal. If things got too serious Mr. Munroe, who was a bit of a wag, was sure to bring everybody back to a cheerful state by saying some funny thing that did not fail to make us all smile. Then Father, who was very exacting in this regard, would invariably take out his watch and say, "Friends, it's time to be on duty and welcome friends and strangers," and so would end the evening meal, a prelude of serious thought and uplifting hope for the work that was to come.[30]

There was plenty of pettiness among these people, as Mrs. Eddy pointed out to them forthrightly on occasion. But there

---

[30] This account occurs in a privately printed work by Johnson ambitiously entitled *The History of the Christian Science Movement*. While this is far from being a reliable, accurate history on the whole, the above-quoted passage has the value of being a firsthand reminiscence.

was also something that lifted them above their ordinary capacities to make them instruments of a movement which within a few years was to girdle the globe—stubborn, quarrelsome, and discouraged disciples sometimes, but steadily putting off the old man and putting on the new.

Again the contrast with Transcendentalism is striking. Remembering the cool graces of an Emerson or an Alcott, we are also reminded of the former's words: "When we see a soul whose acts are regal, graceful, and pleasant as roses, we must thank God that such things can be and are, and not turn sourly on the angel and say: Crump is a better man with his grunting resistance to all his native devils." To which William James later replied: "True enough. Yet Crump may really be the better *Crump*, for his inner discords and second birth; and your once-born 'regal' character, though indeed always better than poor Crump, may fall far short of what he individually might be had he only some Crump-like capacity for compunction over his own peculiar diabolisms, graceful and pleasant and invariably gentlemanly as these may be."

So, in a world of imperfect mortals, Mrs. Eddy preached the command of Jesus: "Be ye therefore perfect, even as your Father which is in heaven is perfect." It seemed to many people that the real force of her movement lay not in her teaching but in her personality—in what Alcott had unflatteringly called her "nervous temperament." The Reverend Stacy Fowler, whose article in the *Homiletic Review* has already been quoted, wrote:

> She [Mrs. Eddy] may teach the principles of the Science in twelve lessons, but she cannot impart her power, her personalism in twelve, nor twelve hundred lessons. The real *ictus* is her personalism. Her pupils are but feeble imitators of their teacher. Hence the spell is losing its charm. The movement is losing its momentum. In its present form it is an epidemic, and

as an epidemic it will pass away, as did the Blue Grass mania. It is as transcendental as was Brook Farm, and like that experiment it may be as useful in demonstrating that sentiment, fancy and fitful impulses are not the solid facts of science, nor the panacea for human ills. . . .

Yet the movement kept growing—by leaps and bounds. Something was wrong in Fowler's analysis. Obviously there was an element of realism in Christian Science which had been lacking in the earlier transcendental intoxication. It is with this historical situation in mind that one can best understand Mrs. Eddy's statement: "Christian Science is no 'Boston craze'; it is the sober second thought of advancing humanity."

6.

Between the years 1889 and 1891 Mrs. Eddy closed down her college, dissolved her church, and retired to Concord, New Hampshire, to spend the next twenty years of her life building for the future. She knew that if her church was to last, it must rest on Principle, not personality. "There was never a religion or philosophy lost to the centuries," she explained, "except by sinking its divine Principle in personality." Again and again she warned against the danger of deifying her personality. The belief that anyone in the flesh was another Christ, she declared, was itself anti-Christ: " 'What went ye out for to see?' A person, or a Principle? Whichever it be, determines the right or wrong of this following."

So her church must be founded on Principle. Always acutely aware of the dangers of organization, she nevertheless recognized that as long as the human mind expresses itself through organic bodies and an organized society, so long would it be necessary for Christian Science to be expressed through an organization to meet the collective as well as individual needs of humanity. In this she again stood in sharp contrast to the anarchic individualism of the Transcendentalists and their amorphous sense of an inspiration unrelated to the problems of collective living. Her church should not founder on the shoals of personal sense, of rival leaderships, of undisciplined idiosyncrasy and selfish atomistic impulses parading as new revelations. It would rest on impersonal law dictated by divine Principle, and it is thus that she regarded the rules and bylaws which comprised her *Manual of The Mother Church.*

Even her harshest critics have paid a certain awestruck tribute to her abilities as an organizer. But Mrs. Eddy's own comment on her achievement gives a revealing glimpse of the nature of the realism which was an inseparable part of her idealism:

> Heaps upon heaps of praise confront me, and for what? That which I said in my heart would never be needed,—namely, laws of limitation for a Christian Scientist. Thy ways are not as ours. Thou knowest best what we need most,—hence my disappointed hope and grateful joy. The redeemed should be happier than the elect. Truth is strong with destiny; it takes life profoundly; it measures the infinite against the finite. Notwithstanding the sacrilegious moth of time, eternity awaits our Church Manual, which will maintain its rank as in the past, amid ministries aggressive and active, and will stand when those have passed to rest.

The reticent dignity of those words gives little hint of the struggles and agonies through which she passed in formulating her necessary "laws of limitation." That part of her life was hidden from the world, which knew her only as a fabulous figure living in quiet seclusion in the "other" Concord. She herself wrote: "Millions may know that I am the Founder of Christian Science. I alone know what that means." And to a clergyman who wrote, asking for an interview, she replied:

Should I give myself the pleasant pastime of seeing your personal self, or give you the opportunity of seeing mine, you would not see me thus, for I am not there. I have risen to look and wait and watch and pray for the spirit of Truth that leadeth away from person—from body to Soul, even to the true image and likeness of God. St. John found Christ, Truth, in the Word which is God. We look for the sainted Revelator in his writings, and there we find him. Those who look for me in person, or elsewhere than in my writings, lose me instead of find me. I hope and trust that you and I may meet in truth and know each other there, and know as we are known of God.

Thus the "fair saint" of Alcott's initial visit in 1876 is best left in the book in which he first encountered her. But what of the *idea* she gave the world? What of the church she left to support it? Institutions have a way of losing sight of their original ideals, of becoming ends in themselves, of ossifying or splintering or withering away. But Mrs. Eddy had noted carefully the pitfalls into which the orthodox Christian churches had fallen. Hers must be different; it must meet the standards of a scientific age; it must furnish *proof* of its claims. "If Christian Science lacked the proof of its goodness and utility," she declared boldly, "it would destroy itself, for it rests alone on demonstration."

Truth, it was clear, must meet the pragmatic test.

CHAPTER THREE

THE PRAGMATIC TEST

I assuredly hold no brief for any of these healers, and must confess that my intellect has been unable to assimilate their theories, so far as I have heard them given. But their *facts* are patent and startling; and anything that interferes with the multiplication of such facts, and with our freest opportunity of observing and studying them, will, I believe, be a public calamity.

WILLIAM JAMES: letter to the
Boston *Transcript* (1894)

Hitherto America has been the land of universal good-will, confidence in life, inexperience of poisons. Until yesterday it believed itself immune from the hereditary plagues of mankind. It could not credit the danger of being suffocated or infected by any sinister principal. The more errors and passions were thrown into the melting-pot, the more certainly would they neutralise one another and would truth come to the top. Every system was met with a frank gaze. "Come on," people seemed to say to it, "show us what you are good for. We accept no claims; we ask for no credentials; we just give you a chance. Plato, the Pope, and Mrs. Eddy shall have one vote each."

GEORGE SANTAYANA: *Character and
Opinion in the United States* (1920)

WHEN JOHN THE BAPTIST sent two of his disciples to Jesus with the question, "Art thou he that should come, or do we look for another?" the Nazarene replied: "Go and show John again those things which ye do hear and see: the blind receive their sight, and the lame walk, the lepers are cleansed, and the deaf hear, the dead are raised up, and the poor have the gospel preached to them. And blessed is he, whosoever shall not be offended in me."

This was a pragmatic answer, and a strain of pure pragmatism runs through the whole New Testament. Luther may

137

have considered the Epistle of James "a right strawy epistle," but to many Christians, dismayed by the great gulf between theological dogma and daily conduct, there is practical sense in the words of James: "Shew me thy faith without thy works, and I will shew thee my faith by my works." Did not the Founder of Christianity himself say: "He that believeth on me, the works that I do shall he do also," and "By their fruits ye shall know them"?

Transcendentalism likewise had its pragmatic strain, beginning with Kant's exaltation of practical reason above pure reason in the attainment of ultimate truth. Coleridge, who did so much to bring German metaphysics to American readers and who remained closer to orthodox Christianity than did most of the New England Transcendentalists, wrote in regard to the Christian teaching: "How can I comprehend this? How is this to be proved? To the first question I should answer: Christianity is not a Theory, or a Speculation; but a *Life*. Not a *Philosophy* of Life, but a Life and a living process. To the second: TRY IT." And elsewhere he wrote: "*Unless ye believe*, says the Prophet, *ye cannot understand*. Suppose (what is at least possible) that the facts should be consequent on the belief, it is clear that without the belief the materials, on which the understanding is to exert itself, would be wanting."

But it was in the United States and in the person of William James that pragmatism emerged as a full-blown philosophy—to become, indeed, *the* American philosophy. It taught that ideas have consequences and that consequences are the test of ideas. It delighted in burgeoning facts rather than fixed principles, in end results rather than first causes. Its universe was unfinished, open, indeterminate, adventurous, pluralistic, on the make. It preferred always the "rich thicket of reality" to the abstract heaven of reason. It would take, said James, "a God who lives in the very dirt of private fact—if that should seem a likely place to find him." It distrusted the noble philosophy whose nobility rested on a careful avoidance of the concrete facts of experience. Of the absolutistic brand of idealism stemming from Hegel, James wrote:

> It keeps no connexion whatever with concreteness. Affirming the Absolute Mind, which is its substitute for God, to be the rational presupposition of all particulars of fact, whatever they may be, it remains supremely indifferent to what the particular facts in our world actually are. . . . Far be it from me to deny the majesty of this conception, or its capacity to yield religious comfort to a most respectable class of minds. But from the human point of view, no one can pretend that it doesn't suffer from the faults of remoteness and abstractness. . . . In this real world of sweat and dirt, it seems to me that when a view of things is "noble," that ought to count as a presumption against its truth, and as a philosophic disqualification. The prince of darkness may be a gentleman, as we are told he is, but whatever the God of earth and heaven is, he can surely be no gentleman. His menial services are needed in the dust of our human trials, even more than his dignity is needed in the empyrean.

It is hardly surprising that James—that "adorable genius," as Whitehead called him—should have been fascinated by the *facts* of mental and spiritual healing. In 1894 he wrote to the Boston *Transcript* protesting the attempt to put legal restrictions on healing methods which were producing such startling new data for empirical examination. Four years later when, in the words of his colleague George Herbert Palmer of Harvard, "the doctors, like trade-unionists, were making one of their periodical assaults on Christian Science," James again stepped forward, this time before the Massachusetts legislature, to argue the case for freedom of spiritual healing. It meant incurring the wrath of the medical fraternity, to which he himself belonged, but his independent stand helped to defeat the restrictive bill the doctors were pushing.

James was well aware of the tendency of scientific thought to erect itself into proscriptive orthodoxies comparable to the religious orthodoxies of the past. "Why do so few 'scientists,'" he asked, "even look at the evidence for telepathy, so called? Because they think, as a leading biologist, now dead, once said to me, that even if such a thing were true, scientists ought to band together to keep it suppressed and concealed. It would undo the uniformity of Nature and all sorts of other things without which scientists cannot carry on their pursuits." He himself declared, with characteristic exuberance: "We must look for the science of the future very often in the dingy and mediumistic corners of the present"—and it was to such a corner that he casually assigned Christian Science, then in its modest and largely misunderstood beginnings. While he never comprehended the metaphysics of Christian Science or even the vast difference between its practice and that of New Thought and the Mental Scientists, his love of the concrete unexpectedness of things enabled him to recognize the fact of Christian Science healing when many of his contemporaries seemed literally incapable of doing so.

Another champion who appeared before the Massachusetts legislature at the same time as James to plead for the freedom of Christian Scientists to practice their religion by healing the sick was William Lloyd Garrison II, son of the old Abolitionist. Bearing eloquent testimony to the results he had seen from the practice of Christian Science, he declared:

> A statement of the truth [about the many failures of orthodox medicine] is not to disparage the noble body of men and women who give their lives and thoughts to this divine service

of humanity, but it is to remind them of their fallibility, and to bespeak their tolerance for others having the same high end. They must know, as every unbiased observer is forced to recognize, that evidences of cures by practitioners not recognized by the "regular schools" abound in this and other communities. The fact must be patent to them because so many of their own patients have found benefit at the hands of mental and other healers whom it is now proposed to disable and drive out. This bill is aimed not at failure but at success. If uniformly bad results came from "irregular practice," the evil would soon stamp itself out. The contrary is the fact, and because of the increasing number who in despair resort to a trial of the new faith, this scheme is launched in the pecuniary interest of the profession. It is in essence the spirit of paternalism, which in trusts and protective laws is everywhere active and hostile to the public weal.

A few years later Benjamin O. Flower, crusading editor of the progressive journal *The Arena,* entered the lists in defense of Christian Science. He had been greatly struck by the comparison in Herbert Spencer's *Social Statics* between the "would-be medical hierarchy" and that of the established church. Spencer had written, somewhat uncharitably: "Moved as are the projectors of a railway, who, whilst secretly hoping for salaries, persuade themselves and others that the proposed railway will be beneficial to the public— moved as all men are under such circumstances, by nine parts of self-interest gilt over with one part of philanthropy— surgeons and physicians are vigorously striving to erect a medical establishment akin to our religious one." Flower, who was half utopian radical, half *laissez-faire* liberal, but wholly committed to the cause of the underdog, saw Christian Science as the victim of this monopolistic tendency.

It should be noted that Christian Scientists themselves have never brought such charges against the doctors. During the eighties when the little movement was under rough attack from outside, Mrs. Eddy permitted herself a splash of defiant rhetoric in her allusion to the "reeling ranks of *materia medica,* with poisons, nostrums, and knives." But her usual references to the medical profession are remarkably appreciative; she speaks of "the cultured class of medical practitioners" as "grand men and women," and declares that "an honest drugging-doctor" is to be preferred to a mental quack. Mature Christian Scientists have generally recognized the self-sacrifice involved in the life of a dedicated doctor, and they have understood how extraordinary and even preposterous their own radical claims must at first seem to someone so deeply drilled in the mechanism of the human body. Hence they have tried to answer the physicians' objections practically rather than polemically. While fighting for their right to practice the healing which must constitute this practical proof, they have been mindful of Mrs. Eddy's words in *Science and Health:*

> Students are advised by the author to be charitable and kind, not only towards differing forms of religion and medicine, but to those who hold these differing opinions. Let us be faithful in pointing the way through Christ, as we understand it, but let us also be careful always to "judge righteous judgment," and never to condemn rashly. "Whosoever shall smite thee on thy right cheek, turn to him the other also." That is, Fear not that he will smite thee again for thy forbearance. If ecclesiastical sects or medical schools turn a deaf ear to the teachings of Christian Science, then part from these opponents as did Abraham when he parted from Lot, and say in thy heart: "Let there be no strife, I pray thee, between me and thee, and between my herdmen and thy herdmen; for we be brethren."

Flower himself pointed out that it was not necessary to assume that the doctors engineering the attack on Christian Science were intentionally dishonest or unfair: "They have, however, been thoroughly educated to believe exactly the opposite of what the Christian Science philosophy teaches." Unconscious prejudice could borrow the vocabulary of scientific objectivity, and rationalization was at least as possible on the part of a doctor attempting to explain away Christian Science cures as on the part of a patient healed by Christian Science after orthodox medical practice had failed to cure him.

The particular incident which called forth Flower's spirited counterattack was the publication in *McClure's Magazine* in August, 1908, of an article by Richard C. Cabot, distinguished Boston physician and professor in the Harvard Medical School. Dr. Cabot's article was entitled "One Hundred Christian Science Cures," and his thesis was that "most Christian Science cures are probably genuine" but "they are not cures of organic disease." Here was set forth the distinction which it has become habitual for medical critics of Christian Science to make—usually as an article of faith rather than as the result of concrete investigation. Christian Science could cure functional but not organic disease. The thesis required a certain amount of elaborate preparation in order to explain away the cases where the evidence pointed to the disease as having been organic. It was necessary to assume that wherever there was a deficiency of clinical evidence available to the investigator to support the original diagnosis the diagnosis was wrong. It was necessary to point out the ambiguous line between organic and functional disease in some cases and to explain that functional disease might sometimes result in serious damage to the organs and tissues of the body. It was necessary to write off some of the cases examined as being beyond scientific determination.

Flower replied by gathering together striking evidence from reputable physicians themselves. One of these— W. F. W. Wilding, a successful British surgeon who later became a Christian Science practitioner—first heard of the new religion through the healing of his father, and his retrospective comment years afterward was illuminating. "The report of this healing," he wrote, "raised such a bitter feeling of resentment in me that I think I should have been more pleased if the cure had failed," for at that time he believed Christian Science to be a form of quackery which had no *right* to heal. However, his opposition was finally broken down when his own daughter, at the point of death, was healed by Christian Science of tuberculosis in both hip joints and in the lungs, from which she had suffered for years under strict medical care; and when several other remarkable cures took place among his patients. Typical of them is the following case, which is chosen for inclusion here because of the brevity with which he recorded it:

> One young man had suffered for about two years from traumatic disease of the knee-joint. This joint was very much enlarged and the various component parts were little else than a mass of pulpy swelling. The surgeons in the infirmary he was attending told him that the only cure was excision of the whole joint, bringing the healthy upper and lower parts of the limb together and letting them unite, leaving him with a leg shortened by several inches and stiff. We surgeons considered this course as a practical success, but the patient felt he would like to keep his whole limb, and therefore turned to those who held out hope to him. He consulted a Christian Science practitioner and was absolutely healed there and then. I myself personally examined this joint the day before and the day after his healing, and can testify to the condition and to the complete healing resulting from one Christian Science treatment.

Another surgeon whom Flower quoted at length was Edmund F. Burton, instructor in the Rush Medical College and a member of the surgical consulting staff of the Cook County Hospital in Chicago. Burton's own healing was spectacular [1] and he also recorded many others which had come to his personal attention, including the healing of inoperable cancer of the stomach. In the last-named case the patient was believed by two nurses in charge of her at the Clara Barton Hospital in Los Angeles to have died, and notation to this effect, together with the hour of death, was made by the head nurse. The patient's brother, who had been asked at the last moment to give her Christian Science treatment, refused to accept the verdict and continued his treatment, with the result that the patient quickly regained consciousness, left the hospital in a day or two, and was soon restored to perfect health.

According to Burton, a "leading Boston physician" (possibly Cabot himself) wrote him skeptically after he had published an article recounting several such healings: "If we can all of us get proof of these statements we must all become Christian Scientists." Burton replied, giving him the names of the attending physicians, supporting affidavits, and other relevant data; but no wholesale conversion of the medical profession followed. It should be noted, however, that in a speech at Harvard seventeen years after his *McClure's* article, Cabot reversed his earlier position, when he declared: "I see no reason why we should admit only one of the different ways through which healing comes to our bodies. I want to take them all, and in that I disagree with Christian Science, the good effects of which I see on all sides. I have not the slightest doubt that it does good, that it cures disease, *organic as well as functional,* only I do not want anybody to say, 'And nothing else cures.' " [2]

Though many doctors have turned to Christian Science through the years, it has more often been through desperate need than through disinterested inquiry. Curiously enough,

---

[1] See Norman Beasley, *The Cross and the Crown,* pp. 503 ff.
[2] *Harvard Alumni Bulletin,* Dec. 31, 1925. Italics added.

there has been little objective scientific investigation of Christian Science healing.[3] While a vast body of testimony has been poured out through the years, skeptics have generally preferred to dismiss the more extraordinary healings as obvious nonsense or the result of misty thinking rather than consider them as possible new data of experience.

In 1917 a French physician, E. Philipon, wrote a thesis on mental healing for the Faculty of Medicine of Paris, with particular attention to the doctrines of Christian Science. This study was later published in the magazine *Science et Vie,* and was followed by a series of articles in which the same author presented various arguments for Christian Science as he understood it—which happened to be with a somewhat Bergsonian flavor. One of these, published in 1919, was in the form of a dialogue between himself and another doctor regarding a collection of testimonies (including ten healings of cancer) presented by Senator John D. Works in a speech in the United States Senate in January, 1915.

Politely but inexorably the other doctor raises the usual objections:

> These accounts first, these assertions, these attestations, these testimonials of sick people cured, or patients who have been helped, do all these things, written from memory sooner or later after the event, merit being considered as documents having real scientific value, as "justifiable cases"? This is doubtful. Many details are lacking in these accounts, many minor details, uninteresting to the sick person but of primary importance to the man of science. And then there are too many adventitious things, too much thanksgiving, too many dithyrambic praises in favor of Mrs. Eddy or Christian Science, many of them probably conscious or unconscious exaggerations, as the human mind is willingly inventive when it comes to a question of its own interest and pride. But these diseases were diag-

---

[3] See Appendix B.

THE PRAGMATIC TEST / 147

nosed? Let us speak of diagnosis. You know as well as I what they are worth, at least most of them. You know how they are made and on what they are founded. Can one with absolute certainty diagnose a deep tumor or attach a name to certain incomplete syndromes? It is possible that our colleagues over the seas, fallible as are all mortals, have been mistaken. They may have called a fibroma a cancer, or named some chronic irritation of the breathing canals tuberculosis; if so, then all that is extraordinary or miraculous in these healings disappears.

Nor is that all. Even suppose the diagnoses are correct, he continues. Who can say definitely that these so-called cures are not mere coincidences and would have occurred anyway? In ordinary medical practice the doctor often asks himself whether this may not be so. "Who tells us, in certain cases, that antipyrine eases our headache, that morphine calms our pain?" Then, in like manner, who tells us that prayer or the Eddy system of treatment has brought about the cures under consideration?

Philipon replies to his friend with Gallic grace and undiminished assurance. He is not at all impressed, he declares, by such arguments. Why complain of the brevity of the testimonies? "It is not a question of specifying the manner of applying the doctrine, of bringing to light its innermost mechanism, but merely of establishing between the healing of the sick and the use of this special treatment a relation of cause to effect." For this a few lines suffice. "The sick begin by indicating the nature of their affliction, then in a few words describe the treatments or the operations undergone, and finish by telling us how as a last resort they tried Christian Science, and the immediate relief or rapid healing that followed." The sincerity of the testifiers is not seriously in question, considering the character and social position of most of those chosen by Senator Works and the certification of their healing by friends, relatives, and doctors. But unconscious exaggeration? "Read over the accounts of healing. Except for the phrases which are almost obligatory, and thus natural, in honor of Christian Science, do you see the least trace of pomposity, of 'literature,' of anything that could sound false or empty to the reader? By no means; all is clearly told, without unnecessary words, or attempts at style or ideas. All those testimonies seem to come from lucid, prudent minds, not given to emotion or mysticism."

But, Philipon continues, his friend has assumed that all this is of no importance because the diagnoses are incorrect. Naturally there are diagnoses that are difficult, some that are impossible to make. "But what does a doctor do in such a case? He remains silent or maintains a prudent reserve. At any rate, he does not, in order to mask his ignorance, advise for his patient a grave operation or a costly treatment." When, as in the examples cited, the doctor prescribes treatment or an operation of that kind, he certainly believes himself sure of his diagnosis. "He can of course be mistaken, but notice that in most of the cases cited by Works, the diagnosis was made not by one but by several doctors: by nine called in consultation in the second testimony . . . ; note that many of these doctors were specialists or professional celebrities, that many times (for instance, cases 1 and 24) examinations were made by which the tumor was seen, felt, and even examined by microscope. The chances of mistake are minimal."

Then there is the question of coincidence. As a general thesis Philipon admits that this can sometimes happen. "Yes, without doubt we cannot say surely if that nervous headache which a moment ago clutched our temples disappeared of itself or gave way to the antipyrine we had taken. We cannot say surely, even if we are perfectly convinced, because banal headache is a malady easily cured, a malady which left to itself always disappears sooner or later." But these cases are different. They are cases of organic disease which would ordinarily be considered [in 1919] incurable or mortal. "It is therefore legitimate to admit that if these maladies are cured it is by virtue of the special treatment, that is to say, of the Christian Science treatment applied." And Philipon concludes:

Altogether, my dear doctor, you see that your criticism cannot resist an impartial examination. Whatever astonishment you may feel about it, you must accustom yourself to this idea of the Invisible, to the obscure but powerful forces which seem to come from the Absolute and which, at the present hour, still appear disordered and wild, but which the doctrine of Christian Science constitutes the first attempt at capturing, the first trial of explanation and synthesis. Yes, besides the objective world we know, besides the world of the senses, there is a subjective world which we barely know, the world of Thought and Soul. A dim world, but with sudden flashes of light, full of vistas towards the Infinite where individual consciousnesses become one yet remain distinct, melting into an ineffable communion but remaining nevertheless separated. Mystics enter there in dreams, but we, the spiritual pioneers, wish to enter in by reason and intelligence, because we feel that to study the Absolute is to modify implicitly the nature and succession of phenomenal series, and that the understanding, however imperfect, of our real being alone can transform the world of appearances.

There is a little too much facility on both sides of this imaginary dialogue, but it suggests some of the blocks which have kept many scientifically minded people from paying serious attention to Christian Science healing—though the situation has been changing markedly in recent years.

One scientific observer who early took the opposite course was Hermann S. Hering, professor of mechanical engineering in the physics department of Johns Hopkins, who attended his first testimony meeting in the 1890's when Christian Science was hardly known. Several of the speakers described healings which seemed quite incredible by ordinary standards. Hering's response was: Either this is a most shameless fraud on the public or there is a new principle here which is of the utmost importance to the world. At the end of the meeting he went up to the testifiers, got their names and addresses, and proceeded to conduct a thorough investigation of their cases until he had satisfied himself in every possible way of the veracity of their accounts. As a result he became convinced that Christian Science had a revolutionary new truth for humanity, devoted himself to its study, became a Christian Science practitioner, teacher, and lecturer, and was called by Mrs. Eddy to Concord, where for several years he had the benefit of her personal direction in his development as a Christian Scientist.

He was only the first of a number of physicists, chemists, engineers, and other scientifically or technically trained men and women to become Christian Scientists. I have been particularly struck in recent years by the number of young Christian Scientists I have met who were engaged in nuclear research or other phases of atomic study. There are Christian Science societies today at Oak Ridge and Los Alamos. On two or three occasions when I have met with the Christian Science Organization at Massachusetts Institute of Technology, composed of students and instructors, I have found that a majority of the keen, healthy young men belonging to the group were doing work in physics, some at an advanced level. As one gets into fields like biology and physical anthropology one encounters fewer Christian Scientists, but in general there are today enough adherents of Christian Science who are trained thoroughly in scientific method and in what constitutes acceptable scientific evidence to make an impressive number. Occasionally such an individual may express a wish that some of his fellow Christian Scientists would report their healings in a more precise style and include the abundant corroborative detail that is often available; but the *fact* of Christian Science healing is to them so irrefutably demonstrable and demonstrated that it outweighs all the uninformed skepticism of the scientific world.

Naturally there are failures in the application of Christian Science—failures which Christian Scientists attribute to their own human shortcomings rather than to any fallibility in the teachings they practice. A few years ago a former physicist, now a Christian Science practitioner, was addressing an interdenominational college group in the Middle West. In the question period at the end, one student asked: "Do I understand you to say that Christian Science can heal *anything?*" Receiving an affirmative reply he continued: "Then why are you wearing glasses?" The Christian Scientist countered by asking: "Would you be willing to tell me what your grades were last term?" "Certainly," replied the student. "All B's." Whereupon the Christian Scientist explained laconically: "Well, I'm wearing glasses for the same reason that you didn't get all A's."

There are no comparative statistics available to show the ratio of Christian Science successes and failures to those of orthodox medicine. However, the legislative recognition given to all aspects of Christian Science practice is a measure of the gradual impression it has made on the community through the years. Even more significant, perhaps, is the special provision made for it by an increasing number of insurance companies. Hundreds of these companies in the United States now recognize Christian Science care in connection with their various casualty lines. Many of them are willing to make the recognition of Christian Science treatment a part of their insurance contracts by issuing endorsements or riders along the following lines:

> It is understood and agreed that wherever the terms "physician" or "surgeon" are used in the attached policy, they shall be deemed to include an authorized Christian Science practitioner of The Mother Church, The First Church of Christ, Scientist, in Boston, Massachusetts. It is further understood and agreed that where the term "hospitalization" is used in this policy, it shall be deemed to include approved Christian Science sanatoriums of this Church, and other nursing homes which may from time to time be approved by the Christian Science Nursing Homes Committee of The Mother Church, and that where the term "professional nursing" is used in this policy it shall be deemed to include nursing by Christian Science nurses authorized by this Church.
>
> By the terms of this rider the [name of the company] shall not be deemed to have waived its right and opportunity to examine the person of the insured when and so often as it may reasonably require during the pendency of any claim hereunder, or at any other time.[4]

The significance of this special recognition of Christian Science lies in its wholly pragmatic basis. It cannot be written off as a triumph of ecclesiastical propaganda or public relations, and certainly not as an evidence of the insurance companies' abstract respect for religious rights. As American businessmen delight to say, they are not in the business "for their health." Christian Science treatment must pay off before they will recognize it. Here in a tangible, literal way is a proof of what William James called the "cash value" of an

---

[4] It is worth noting that Mrs. Eddy's organization, The Mother Church, with its system of authorizing or approving Christian Science practitioners, nurses, and nursing homes (where practical care but no medication is available to patients who may need such care during the course of a healing), receives recognition as something of a guarantee of the quality or correctness of the treatment administered.

idea. Here is Christian Science reduced to its most elementary terms of pragmatic usefulness.

2.

Before leaving the question of physical healing, it is necessary to take account of changes that have occurred outside of Christian Science since Mrs. Eddy first proclaimed her gospel. In this century the whole situation in regard to the treatment of disease has altered. Medicine and surgery have made sensational advances which have caused them to look back at the medical practice of a few decades ago as to an archaic and benighted art—though the doctors of 1900 or 1919 censored Christian Science with as much confidence in their own position as the most up-to-date specialist of today.

At the same time psychoanalysis and psychosomatic medicine have deeply shaken the foundations of orthodox medicine. The lines between organic and functional disease have become far more wavering than in Cabot's day. Since Sauerbruch declared that "perhaps the purely bacteriological and serological conception of disease may have led medical science into a blind alley," one disease after another has come to be assigned a psychosomatic basis—stomach ulcers; high blood pressure; diseases of the heart, the colon, and the skin; thyroid disturbances; rheumatism; asthma; diabetes. In 1957 the annual meeting of the National Tuberculosis Association was reminded by one of its speakers of the great Osler's statement: "What goes on in the patient's mind is more important than what goes on in his chest." The year before, two physicians from the New York Hospital-Cornell Medical Center had reported at the annual meeting of the American Medical Association that experimental studies revealed no basis for assuming that some diseases are psychosomatic while others are not, since there is no part of the human system which may not be affected by the way a person reacts to life situations.

Experiments have been made in which hypnotized individuals have been given powerful drugs that ordinarily produce certain well-defined reactions in the human organism, but the hypnotist has told his subject that the drug administered would produce exactly the opposite reaction; the results have followed the hypnotist's suggestion and not the drug's normal action. One popular writer on psychosomatic medicine, Dr. Frank G. Slaughter, commenting on the many busy and successful doctors who treat practically everything with injections of vitamins, drugs, or hormones, declares that in the vast majority of cases "an injection of sterilized water would have much the same effect, if it was accompanied by the assurance of the doctor that it was particularly good for the patient's symptoms." [5]

Another doctor, Ian Stevenson, engaged in research into the psychosomatic aspects of heart disease, writes of the striking specialization that has marked modern medicine: "Today we pay for our knowledge of the parts in ignorance of the whole"—a comment which might be extended to the piecemeal empiricism of a positivistic age in other directions than medicine. And speaking of the training of physicians, he declares: "Studies which might humanize the student are jostled aside to make room for courses so restricted in content as to make him, frequently, a sort of scientific barbarian, unaware of the truth of Professor Clark Kennedy's dictum: 'In medicine we are bound to deal with human life and experience as a whole, and half the art of medicine is to adopt a reasonable and practical attitude to the unknown.' " [6]

Various well-informed writers have pointed out the enormous amount of unnecessary and sometimes dangerous sur-

---

[5] *Medicine for Moderns,* (New York, Julian Messner, 1947), p. 191.
[6] "Why Medicine Is Not a Science," *Harper's Magazine,* April, 1949.

gery performed because surgeons are unaware of the mental and emotional bases of the complaints for which they operate. In a review of the book *Psychosomatic Medicine*, by Edward Weiss, M.D., and O. Spurgeon English, M.D., Dr. Walter C. Alvarez of the Mayo Clinic writes: "Without the knowledge contained within the covers of this book a man able to do surgery is a dangerous person to let loose in a community."

Typical of the changing attitudes of specialists of many sorts are the remarks made by Dr. Loring T. Swain when President of the American Rheumatism Association and Secretary of the Pan-American League for the Study and Control of Rheumatic Diseases:

> From accumulating experience I am convinced that there are spiritual laws which will change lives if they are scientifically applied to the actual problems of life, and a new philosophy results. My study of patients makes me believe that all forms of selfishness point to a starved, undeveloped spiritual life. . . . You may ask what are the results on arthritis of this spiritual approach. It does not always cure the arthritis or restore the joints to normal, but it is an essential factor, a factor without which the patient cannot advance beyond a certain point.

This is all a far cry from the mechanistic concepts which dominated the field when Mrs. Eddy threw down her revolutionary challenge. Today there is a tendency among medical historians to describe her work as that of a pioneer in the field of mental healing—a sort of brilliant amateur, haphazardly hitting on principles which, they sometimes assume, have now been brought to a point of scientific precision through the development of depth analysis. There is one great difficulty with this. If Christian Scientists are judged by their actual healings, then their performance is seen to be so far in advance of the laborious therapeutic techniques of the psychotherapists that it may be questioned whether the latter have even glimpsed the scientific principle involved in Christian Science healing.

Those who practice Christian Science are grateful for the startling growth in public recognition of the mental and emotional factors in disease, but the analyst's technique seems to them scarcely closer to their own than is that of "the honest drugging-doctor." He is still operating within the field of "mortal mind," manipulating secondary factors rather than laying hold of that primary power which modifies "the nature and succession of phenomenal series."

It is this basic difference which prevents the Christian Scientist from carrying on his healings in the sort of experimental, laboratory atmosphere which the scientific investigator demands. Because healing is a by-product of his communion with God he cannot undertake to make any given case a controlled experiment, inviting the physician or psychiatrist to check its course day by day or even before and after. It often happens that physical examinations, including X-rays and microscope tests, are made before or after a healing—under the supervision of insurance companies, school authorities, Army doctors, or at the request of anxious relatives or business firms which insist on such examinations before an employee can be reinstated, but not normally at the patient's own volition. The faithful Christian Scientist's position must always be that his health is a reflection of his unity with God and that no physical evidence, either pro or con, can bear witness to his true status as the son of God. Physical health is to him not an end in itself, to be established and verified by material processes; it is one of the added things of which Jesus spoke when he said: "Seek ye first the kingdom of God, and his righteousness; and all these things shall be added unto you." To undertake a healing as a controlled experiment would violate this basic rule;

it would even savor a little of Satan's temptation to the Saviour to cast himself down from the pinnacle of the temple as a dramatic demonstration of God's power to save.

A rational light is thrown on this whole subject by a little-known but profoundly searching book, *The Resurrection Pattern*, by Geoffrey Hoyland (London, Gerald Duckworth & Co., 1947). Mr. Hoyland writes as an intelligent layman in the fields of science and religion. His book expresses a pure, translucent Christianity which stops short of the all-embracing metaphysical logic of Christian Science but accepts spiritual healing as a valid scientific phenomenon. Of the means of measuring this phenomenon he writes:

> We are confined almost exclusively to the historical method . . . since the higher spiritual forces do not lend themselves to normal scientific treatment; we cannot lay on faith, love, and holiness in a laboratory, to be used as desired, in the same way that we can provide water, electricity, and sulphuretted hydrogen. We can usually only investigate events that have already happened, with all the uncertainty that such historical methods imply.

But "miracles," he points out, have happened in the best-regulated scientific families, and he gives a readily recognizable and immensely suggestive example. Suppose that a small boy is playing with tin tacks and a small bar of steel. The boy picks up the tacks from the table and lets them go; they immediately fall back—"pulled down thither by the attractive force of the earth, according to Newton, and pursuing their natural geodetic lines through the space-time continuum (bent into the fourth dimension by the near mass of our planet) according to Einstein." Then the boy holds the bar of steel a fraction of an inch above one of the tacks on the table, and the miracle happens. Instead of remaining inert on the table—"as it should have done according to the gravitation laws of both systems"—the tack leaps up in the air and adheres to the steel bar.

We do not regard this as a miracle because we have discovered the natural laws and forces in accordance with which this phenomenon takes places, yet it is miraculous in relation to gravitation regarded as a closed system. In the same way spiritual healing lies beyond the explanations of either gravitation or electromagnetism. Natural science is further hampered in approaching it by the fact that it possesses no instruments to measure the higher spiritual forces. Mr. Hoyland comments:

We may, perhaps, gather some idea of what this handicap entails by considering how we should attempt to convince a sceptical "gravitationist" of the existence of the terrestrial magnetic field within the four walls of an ordinary house *if the use of a magnetic compass, or other sensitive instrument, were denied to us.* We might assure him that every steel object was slightly affected, but he would remain incredulous. We might tell him that when he held a penknife aloft and let it fall upon the carpet its path downward was deflected, even though infinitesimally, by the magnetic field, but he would still be unconvinced. "I can see no evidence whatever to support your theory," he might reply; "Such slight deflections as you think you can detect are perfectly well explainable by natural causes, such as the faint air-currents in the room. This magnetic theory of yours is pure superstition, there is no positive proof of its existence." The expert in magnetism, who had listened to this dispute, would have a different story to tell. . . . "I can state positively, on purely theoretical grounds, that *every* steel object in the house is affected by the magnetic field and its geodetic modified to some extent thereby. I am perfectly aware that this effect is too small to be observed by your gross senses and that other causes, such as the gravitationist's suggested air-currents, may be more than enough to explain everything you may observe, or think you observe, when you drop pen-knives on the floor or spin the cutlery on the dining-room table, but this does not affect my argument in the least. I am convinced of the real existence of the magnetic field and therefore I *know* that the effect exists. . . ."

This certainly is not mere dogmatism; it can be validated today not merely with tin tacks but with all the stupendous achievements that the utilization of electromagnetism has made possible. Yet the theoretical understanding preceded the technological applications; the real scientific achievement was the discovery of a principle rather than the practical results flowing from it.

In an analogous way the Christian Scientist testifies to a healing which he regards as the outward evidence of an inner illumination; but to him the real healing is the change of thought, the better understanding he gains of God and of his true relationship to Him. He sees his religion as a pure science as well as an applied one. *Perfecta scientia Deum scire.* Ye shall know the truth, and—only then—the truth shall make you free. If Christian Science were a mere healing cult, if ease in matter were its aim, a Christian Scientist would be justified in trying one of the so-called miracle drugs if he did not receive an immediate healing from spiritual treatment; but many testifiers express particular gratitude for the spiritualization of thought and regeneration of character that have taken place during a slow, protracted healing. Others tell of receiving instantaneous healings at the moment at which they finally dropped all desire for mere physical well-being and turned with their whole heart and soul to know God as the source and substance of all true being.

The published testimonies of Christian Science healing provide a wealth of case histories for anyone seriously interested in tracing the connection between spiritual regeneration and physical healing. A large body of evidence supports the emphasis made by Mrs. Eddy in an often-quoted passage from *Science and Health:*

> To-day the healing power of Truth is widely demonstrated as an immanent, eternal Science, instead of a phenomenal exhibition. Its appearing is the coming anew of the gospel of "on earth peace, good-will toward men." This coming, as was promised by the Master, is for its establishment as a permanent dispensation among men; but the mission of Christian Science now, as in the time of its earlier demonstration, is not primarily one of physical healing. Now, as then, signs and wonders are wrought in the metaphysical healing of physical disease; but these signs are only to demonstrate its divine origin,—to attest the reality of the higher mission of the Christ-power to take away the sins of the world.

This quotation leads us to one of the most striking developments of recent years: the remarkable growth of interest in spiritual healing in the historic Christian churches. Mrs. Eddy once predicted that if the lives of Christian Scientists attested their fidelity to Truth, the Christian churches of the United States and some other countries would, within the twentieth century, approximate the understanding of Christian Science sufficiently to heal the sick in Christ's name. This prophecy appears within measurable distance of realization, if the word *approximate*—both as to healing results and metaphysical understanding—be stressed.

The pioneer effort of the Protestant churches to meet the Christian Science challenge was the Emmanuel Movement within the Episcopal Church. It was started in Boston in the early 1900's by two Episcopal clergymen, in an avowed effort to show that healing was possible within the traditional Christian framework. Out of the movement emerged Dr. Lyman P. Powell, for many years rector of St. Margaret's in New York City, who was later to become an outspoken champion for Mrs. Eddy. Though the Emmanuel Movement as such declined in importance with the years, it gave impetus to tendencies and aspirations which have come into notable evidence in Protestantism recently.

One major denomination after another has made official pronouncements on the necessity of restoring to the Church the healing of bodily ills which the Founder of Christianity made an integral part of the salvation he preached. Healing services are held regularly in many churches of many faiths. The Church of England has set a pattern which has been followed by other denominations in establishing its Archbishops' Commission on Divine Healing, composed of clerics, doctors, and psychiatrists, to conduct a serious and prolonged study of the whole subject.

No longer is it considered a sign of religious bad taste to draw attention to the important part played by healing in the New Testament. One is reminded a little ironically of the statement by the Harvard biologist, Louis Agassiz, quoted by Mrs. Eddy: "Every great scientific truth goes through three stages. First, people say it conflicts with the Bible. Next, they say it has been discovered before. Lastly, they say they have always believed it." This is an especially appropriate commentary on those surveys of healing in the modern church that manage virtually to ignore the woman, the book, and the movement that have unquestionably done more than all else to restore Christian healing to the world. However, many Protestant clergymen have paid generous tribute to the part played by Christian Science in this resurgence of interest in healing, and several eminent clerics have gone so far as to state publicly that they believe Mrs. Eddy was divinely commissioned to bring the Christian church back to its neglected duty to save the *whole* man.

The vast majority of striking cures accomplished within

the Protestant church—not to mention such Roman Catholic phenomena as the miracles at Lourdes—can be classified as simple faith healings. This includes everything from the "laying on of hands" in the primitive Pentecostal sects to the sophisticated activities of Episcopal clergymen working clinically with physicians and psychiatrists. In some cases there is exclusive reliance on prayer for healing; in others prayer may be combined with drugs, placebos, and hypnotism. The general tendency is to see God as working through many means for the cure of the body; and however much metaphysical and philosophical confusion there may be in such a conception, it allows for faith to be divided between spiritual and material means without any sense of inconsistency. Moreover, where the healing is looked on as a "miracle" or special intervention of Deity, setting aside the normal processes of nature established by that same Deity, there need not be any reluctance to employ medical means or invite medical observation, since the normal processes are still believed to hold good unless and until a miracle occurs.

All of this contrasts markedly with Christian Science, which cannot be combined with material means for the simple reason that it is not a mere *faith* but a total view of life, a radical metaphysic which requires that faith become understanding if healing is to be genuinely scientific. The stubborn, irreducible facts of experience have shown that under ordinary circumstances any attempt to mix Christian Science and medicine seriously lessens the efficacy of each.

Thus the Christian Scientist still occupies a unique place in the spectrum of spiritual healing. It is for him the indispensable sign of a revolutionary approach to life—a *healing* approach which extends immeasurably beyond the range of bodily well-being. He welcomes with pleasure the growing recognition within the orthodox churches that there is no earthly condition beyond the reach of God's healing power, but he finds the key to this power in a metaphysical position that is still radically in advance of most Protestant doctrine.[7]

3.

Mrs. Eddy has written in *Rudimental Divine Science:* "Healing physical sickness is the smallest part of Christian Science. It is only the bugle-call to thought and action, in the higher range of infinite goodness." Unquestionably the majority of Christian Scientists, except among second-, third-, and fourth-generation adherents, have initially been drawn to it by the need for healing. And even if the purpose of the bugle-call is to summon them to loftier tasks, it is still important that the call itself shall be clear, loud, and unwavering in its summons. Nevertheless, the higher range stretches out ahead. All the poverty and frustration, the sin and violence of human life cry out for healing. A world where the individual seems engulfed in the mass, where things are in the saddle and ride mankind, must be redeemed in the interests of truth and beauty and the spiritual dignity of man.

At the same time the positivistic challenge must be met at every level. More than blind faith is necessary to surmount our giant problems; we need a scientific understanding of the whole in order to cope with our technical knowledge of the parts. Even pragmatism recognizes that more than piecemeal demonstration of truth is necessary. William James wrote: "If theological ideas prove to have a value for concrete life, they will be true, for pragmatism, in the sense of being good for so much. For how much more they are true, will depend entirely on their relations to the other truths that also have

---

[7] A useful survey of the present status of spiritual healing in the churches is A. Graham Ikin's *New Concepts of Healing* (New York, Association Press, 1956), which includes in an appendix an authoritative statement of the Christian Science position.

to be acknowledged." An ultimate coherence stands above any particular utility as the test of truth.

The Founder of Christianity himself made this clear when he said: "Many will say to me in that day, Lord, Lord, have we not prophesied in thy name? and in thy name have cast out devils? and in thy name done many wonderful works? And then will I profess unto them, I never knew you: depart from me, ye that work iniquity." Here is implied a distinction between "wonderful works" which answer to the definition of magic given by modern anthropologists as an attempt to "use" divine powers to fulfill selfish human ends, and those that follow from a knowledge of and conformity to God's will, or the nature of reality.

An interesting reminder of Mrs. Eddy's early awareness of the higher purpose of Christian Science occurred at the time of the dedication of the huge new edifice of The Mother Church in 1906, when thousands of Christian Scientists poured into Boston for the occasion. The press of the world was staggered at this sign of so great a vitality in so new a religion. Mrs. Eddy's biographer, Sibyl Wilbur, writes of it:

> The Christian Scientists who had come to Boston to see The Mother Church dedicated remained to attend the Wednesday evening meeting at which testimonies of Christian Science healing were given. The great temple was crowded from floor to dome, and overflow meetings were held in the original Mother Church and in four public halls. Many who were not Christian Scientists were amazed listeners to the outpouring of testimonies from every part of the great auditorium. Men and women arose in their places on the floor of the church and in the first and second balconies. As each arose he called the name of his city and waited his turn to tell of the miracle of health and virtue wrought in his life as a result of the study of Christian Science. The names of the cities called up the near and far of the civilized world—Liverpool, Galveston, St. Petersburg,

San Francisco, Paris, New York, Atlanta, and Portland. There were Negroes as well as white men in that audience; there were French, German, and Scandinavian; there were army officers from Great Britain, and members of the British nobility, Americans of great wealth, jurists, former doctors and clergymen, teachers, clerks, day laborers. It was like a jubilation of an army with banners. And not only of the vanquishment of cancers, consumption, broken limbs, malignant diseases, and paralysis did these votaries of Christian Science testify, but of poverty overcome, victory gained over drunkenness, morphine, and immoral lives. It was a triumphant assertion of the health and power of spiritual living.[8]

This was fine, but it was not enough. A deeper hint is found in a letter written to Mrs. Eddy on this occasion by S. P. Bancroft, who had studied with her in 1870 and had been present when Bronson Alcott visited her little group six years later. His letter started:

My Dear Teacher:
Of the many thousands who attended the dedicatory services at the Christian Science church last Sunday it is doubtful if there was one so deeply impressed with the grandeur and magnitude of your work as was the writer, whom you will recall as a member of your *first* class in Lynn, Mass., nearly forty years ago. When you told us that the truth you expounded was the little leaven that should leaven the whole lump, we thought this might be true in some far distant day beyond our mortal vision. It was above conception that in less than forty years a new system of faith and worship, as well as of healing, should number its adherents by the hundreds of thousands and its tenets be accepted wholly or in part by nearly every religious and scientific body in the civilized world.

The last part of the last sentence soars dizzily beyond the

---

[8] Sibyl Wilbur, *The Life of Mary Baker Eddy* (Boston, The Christian Science Publishing Society, 1938), p. 342 f.

facts, but is an understandable exaggeration in view of the enthusiasm engendered by the occasion. He continues:

> Seated in the gallery of that magnificent temple, which has been reared by you, gazing across that sea of heads, listening again to your words explaining the Scriptures, my mind was carried back to that first public meeting in the little hall on Market Street, Lynn, where you preached to a handful of people that would scarce fill a couple of pews in this grand amphitheatre; and as I heard the sonorous tones of the powerful organ and the mighty chorus of five thousand voices, I thought of the little melodeon on which my wife played, and of my own feeble attempts to lead the singing. . . . No human being in this generation has accomplished such a work or been so thoroughly endorsed or so completely vindicated. It is marvellous beyond all imagining to one who knew of your early struggles.

He reminds her of the words of his uncle, a deacon of the First Congregational Church of Lynn, when the good man heard that he had studied with Mrs. Eddy: "My boy, you will be ruined for life; it is the work of the devil." And he concludes with another reminder which holds the clue to the whole development of Christian Science as a serious contestant for the attention of thinking men and women: "I have yet the little Bible which you gave me as a reward for the best paper on the spiritual significance of the first chapter of Genesis. It has this inscription on the fly-leaf in your handwriting, 'With all thy getting get understanding.'" [9]

Get understanding! Here is the key to Mrs. Eddy's own life and to the continuing growth of Christian Science. In her years of so-called retirement at Concord her mental horizon was constantly widening. Her active interest darted in many directions; her thinking grew in scope and depth.

---

[9] This letter is quoted in *The First Church of Christ, Scientist, and Miscellany,* by Mary Baker Eddy, p. 58 f.

The visitors who came to her there were often people of much larger stature and broader culture than her associates of past years, and she reached out mentally to far parts of the world and generations yet unborn.

At the same time the attacks on her in the press grew fierce and frequent. Mark Twain, torn between his concept of her as a self-deluded charlatan and his persistent admiration for her as in several ways "the most interesting woman that ever lived" and "the benefactor of the age," lashed out against a faith that *almost* convinced him, but passed the eminently pragmatic judgment: "When we do not know a person—and also when we do—we have to judge his size by the size and nature of his achievements, as compared with the achievements of others in his special line of business—there is no other way. Measured by this standard, it is thirteen hundred years since the world has produced anyone who could reach up to Mrs. Eddy's waistbelt." [10] Less pragmatic was the judgment passed by that exquisite Brahmin, Charles Eliot Norton, who could hail *Leaves of Grass* in 1855 as harmoniously fusing "Yankee transcendentalism and New York rowdyism," yet half a century later spoke with the desiccated accents of the genteel tradition when he declared: "Mother Eddy is the most striking and ugliest figure in New England today." [11]

Such a judgment is less surprising when one remembers the picture of senility, cupidity, and ignorant fanaticism which was presented to the public through much of the press

---

[10] See *Awake to a Perfect Day,* by Clara Clemens (New York, Citadel Press, 1956), for a revealing picture of her father's changing attitude toward Christian Science and Mrs. Eddy.

[11] See, however, *Mary Baker Eddy and Her Books,* by William Dana Orcutt (Boston, The Christian Science Publishing Society, 1950) for a vastly different firsthand estimate by a friend and disciple of Norton. Especially interesting in the light of Norton's aesthetic standards are Mrs. Eddy's perceptive comments on William Morris and the Kelmscott Chaucer as recorded by Orcutt, pp. 68 ff.

as a portrait of Mrs. Eddy—to be reproduced almost verbatim by unscrupulous later biographers. A very different picture was drawn by the psychiatrist Allan McLane Hamilton, grandson of Alexander Hamilton, Fellow of the Royal Society of Edinburgh, founder of the Psychiatrical Society, and universally regarded as one of the most reliable and independent experts on mental disease in the United States. Called to examine Mrs. Eddy's mental competence in connection with the Next Friends' Suit in 1907, when she was eighty-six years old, he spoke in his official report of the "inherent evidences of mental vigor" in her letters, of their "intellectual good order," and of her "capacity to appreciate details [and] to correct mistakes." In a subsequent interview published in the New York *Times* on August 25, 1907, he gave an expanded account of his personal impression of her:

> I was immediately impressed with the extraordinary intelligence shown in her eyes. In aged persons the eyes are apt to appear dimmed, contracted, and lacking in expression. With Mrs. Eddy, however, they are large, dark, and at times almost luminous in appearance.
>
> As she talked to me, or answered my questions, the play of expression on her features evinced unusual intelligence, and was in strict keeping with what she said. Her whole bearing was dignified and reserved, in perfect accord with what one would expect in a woman of education and refinement. . . .
>
> I must confess that I approached this conference with Mrs. Eddy in a decidedly prejudiced state of mind. I had read the current abuse of her that one finds in the magazines and newspapers, and from this reading had become imbued with a distinctly adverse feeling toward Christian Science and its chief exponent. But when I saw and talked with the latter, and read and analyzed her correspondence, I experienced a complete revulsion of feeling, and this to such an extent that I have now become candidly of the opinion that Mrs. Eddy is not only sincere in all she says and does, but I believe, also, that she

unselfishly spends her money for the perpetuation of a church which, in her estimation, is destined to play an important part in the betterment of humanity—nor have I found that she is guilty of any extravagant indulgences such as one might look for were her motives less pure. . . .

For a woman of her age I do not hesitate to say that she is physically and mentally phenomenal. In the matter of her longevity, some Christian Scientists have gone so far as to assert that she will never die. She herself, however, does not hold to any such ridiculous belief, but refers frequently to the life after death as a state of existence to which she is liable. I fancy that the belief among some of her followers involving the indefinite continuance of her earthly life arises purely from the visible evidence of Mrs. Eddy's great vitality and absence of any of the usual tokens of mental breakdown natural to one of her great age.

The most remarkable evidence of this vitality—which was, to her more comprehending followers, the vitality of an idea rather than of a person—occurred a year later, after she had moved from Concord to Chestnut Hill, outside Boston. There she started *The Christian Science Monitor*. By this act she brought Christian Scientists face to face with the larger world that lay beyond their personal experience and challenged them to heal it as they would a sick patient.

Her thoughts had long been moving in this direction. Her interest in public affairs grew keener with the years. In 1899, at the brink of the new century, she had warned her followers, quite in the spirit of William Jennings Bryan: "I reluctantly foresee great danger threatening our nation,— imperialism, monopoly, and a lax system of religion." The next year in the New York *World* she warned against "industrial slavery" and "insufficient freedom of honest competition." Though she herself never moved into the field of social criticism or political action, she became increasingly aware of the need to provide a means by which Christian Science thinking could be educated up to its larger responsibilities and by which the vision of reality furnished by Christian Science could flow out "for the healing of the nations."

Few of her followers at first caught the magnitude of her intention. In the early years of the *Monitor* the emphasis was frequently put on its "wholesomeness," its freedom from sensationalism and from the crass exploitation of crime and disaster. This was a legitimate virtue to point to, but a negative one. It was something of the emphasis she herself had given, back in 1883, when she wrote that "a newspaper edited and published by the Christian Scientists has become a necessity." At that time she had declared: "Looking over the newspapers of the day, one naturally reflects that it is dangerous to live, so loaded with disease seems the very air. These descriptions carry fears to many minds, to be depicted in some future time upon the body. A periodical of our own will counteract to some extent this public nuisance; for through our paper, at the price at which we shall issue it, we shall be able to reach many homes with healing, purifying thought."

This statement, however, introduced the monthly *Christian Science Journal* with its natural emphasis on bodily healing as the outward sign of an inward and individual regeneration. Twenty-five crowded years were to elapse before Mrs. Eddy was ready to found the periodical which should concern itself, though in a less explicit way, with the healing of the body politic.

In January, 1908, she moved from Concord to Chestnut Hill for the last three years of her life, and was thus near enough to Boston to keep in close touch with the newspaper which she founded later in the year. A proof of the editorial page was taken out to her home each day for her release. A noted English journalist who was brought from London to help get the paper started wrote later: "Mrs. Eddy herself took the utmost interest in everything, and, from the moment the first number was issued, actively guided the policy and destiny of the paper as it rapidly grew into an organ with a great circulation embracing every country in the world." [12]

"The object of the *Monitor*," she wrote in the leading editorial of the first issue on November 25, 1908, "is to injure no man, but to bless all mankind." In a less frequently quoted phrase she also defined its purpose "to spread undivided the Science that operates unspent." [13] Christian Science could not spend itself on the problems of the individual and ignore those great collective issues which are indivisibly bound up with individual welfare. Of Jesus, the Exemplar, she had written in *Science and Health:* "His mission was both individual and collective." In the same book she declared: "Happiness is spiritual, born of Truth and Love. It is unselfish; therefore it cannot exist alone, but requires all mankind to share it." And elsewhere she wrote that only in a state of evil thinking "can we in belief separate one man's interests from those of the whole human family." [14]

---

[12] Frederick Dixon in the *Outlook* (London). Quoted in *Editorial Comments on the Life and Work of Mary Baker Eddy* (Boston, The Christian Science Publishing Society, 1911).

[13] The phrase is adapted from a passage in Pope's *Essay on Man* which deeply impressed Mrs. Eddy as a girl, and which echoed in many of her phrases in later years:

> All are but parts of one stupendous whole,
> Whose body Nature is, and God the soul;
> That, chang'd through all, and yet in all the same;
> Great in the earth, as in th' etherial frame;
> Warms in the sun, refreshes in the breeze,
> Glows in the stars, and blossoms in the trees,
> Lives through all life, extends through all extent,
> Spreads undivided, operates unspent.

[14] See "Our Individual and Collective Mission," by Herbert E. Rieke, *The Christian Science Journal*, Nov., 1947, and "An Individual and Collective Mission," by Anne S. Peel, *Christian Science Sentinel*, May 14, 1955.

It would have been very easy for some Christian Scientists, motivated by an unconscious escapism disguised as a lofty metaphysical purity, to turn their backs on the evils beyond their own immediate experience on the merely dialectical ground that such evils are no part of God's perfect creation and are therefore unreal. But ignoring or evading evil is no part of the *modus operandi* of Christian Science healing. The specific truth must be seen about a specific error in order to destroy it. Mrs. Eddy's founding of the *Monitor*, which she considered her greatest single achievement after the writing of *Science and Health*, forced the conscientious Christian Scientist to begin a purification of his own social and political attitudes through letting the transforming Christ-spirit into his thinking about these matters.

Many a Christian Scientist has borne witness to the healing of a personal problem when he has enlarged his prayer to embrace the world. The individual immersed in his own ailments is admonished by Mrs. Eddy: "We should forget our bodies in remembering good and the human race." Some Christian Scientists still fail to recognize the deep significance played in the development of Christian Science by her founding of the *Monitor*, but her more alert followers began gradually to understand the challenge. A month after the first issue appeared, one of her students wrote in the *Christian Science Sentinel:*

> Our Leader's request that "every Christian Scientist . . . subscribe for and read our daily newspaper" (*Sentinel*, Nov. 21) is a call to a higher privilege, and the significance of this request is gradually assuming more and more definite proportions. . . . The first conspicuous effect of this wonderful gift to ourselves and to the world has been to lift one's eyes to an horizon far beyond one's own doorstep. The call to help in the world's thinking is no longer something that can pass unheeded, it is an imperative duty. Things we did not like to look at nor think

of, problems we did not feel able to cope with, must now be faced manfully, and correct thinking concerning the world's doings cultivated and maintained.

It may be asked why this result could not have been achieved as well by encouraging Christian Scientists to read other good newspapers and keep themselves generally informed of the world's grievous needs. As a matter of fact, most Christian Scientists do read regularly a local newspaper as well as the *Monitor,* and many keep themselves well informed through all the normal channels of information. But the *Monitor's* uniqueness lies in the fact that it approaches every problem with the basic purpose of healing.

It encourages at the same time that it enlightens. While it reports the unhealed evil in the world objectively and impartially, it tries to keep this in reasonable perspective with the active good. In even the darkest situation it seeks editorially to discover the point at which positive action may be effective. It frequently warns of the unhappy effects that may result from a situation unless it is drastically corrected, but it never abandons itself to the luxury of wringing its hands in debilitating despair over the turn of events. It plays the role neither of Cassandra nor of Pollyanna, but attempts to combine a humanly realistic appraisal of events with that deeper realism which recognizes no human situation as beyond redemption by the divine intelligence and love available to man as the reflection of God.

It cannot be said that all Christian Scientists appreciate either the purpose or the achievement of the *Monitor.* In some cases indifference or prejudice blinds them to its merits, but it stands there nevertheless as a challenge to their loyalty and serves a major educational purpose within the Christian Science movement as a whole. Some Christian Scientists are first awakened to the importance of their daily paper by seeing the enormous respect it has won in the world at large. Among statesmen, educators, and journalists throughout the world the *Monitor* enjoys a remarkable prestige. Sir Winston Churchill has repeatedly paid tribute to it, speaking of it as occupying the same high place in American life that the Manchester *Guardian* does in British, and the Soviet Union's Mr. Molotov, at the height of his international activity, referred to it, more curiously, as the only *serious* American newspaper.

Actually it does not intend to be an "American" newspaper but an international one. Since most of its staff and a large majority of its readers are American, this fact is obviously reflected, consciously and unconsciously, in its columns; but its center of gravity is not to be defined in national, geographical, political, economic, or social terms. It starts from the concept of fundamental reality as being wholly spiritual, the expression of a divine Principle which is not to be identified with any particular historical development or human institution. Since Spirit is the sole reality, in the Christian Science view, all human institutions are relative, temporal, powerless of themselves to ensure justice, peace, or plenty.

This does not make for a nihilistic view of society. It invites a constant examination to determine where the greatest measure of Principle may be expressed in any given combination of circumstances. It supports the highest relative good it can find in persons and policies—in line with Mrs. Eddy's statement: "Wisdom in human action begins with what is nearest right under the circumstances, and thence achieves the absolute"—but it avoids doctrinaire alignment with any party or program, finding an element of fallibility in all of them. It does not attempt to dictate opinions to its readers, or to Christian Scientists in general, or to set forth an "official" Christian Science view on politi-

cal and social questions. It encourages an essentially pragmatic play of free-wheeling intelligence among human
affairs, because the only absolute it accepts is wholly above
the flux of history, an inexhaustible source of the intelligence
necessary to order affairs harmoniously but not committed
to any one limited pattern of progress.

I am speaking here, of course, of the ideal attitude possible to *The Christian Science Monitor;* I am not suggesting
that it always lives up to that ideal, any more than the individual Christian Scientist always and completely demonstrates the teachings to which he is committed. Since the
Monitor is edited and staffed by fallible human beings (however consecrated to their ideal) and is subject to contemporary pressures (however much freer in this respect than
many newspapers) it would be surprising if it did not sometimes show failures of prescience or courage or disinterested
intelligence. What is perhaps more surprising is the wide-
spread opinion among well-informed people to both the left
and the right of it that, even when they disagree with its
editorial judgments, it remains a model of decency and sanity in a violent, chaotic world.

Does this make it, by any chance, a mere survival of the
Age of Reason existing on wishful thinking in the Age of
Anxiety? Is this sort of enlightenment no more than a momentary glow in the dying embers of nineteenth-century
liberalism? The test which all forms of liberalism must meet
in this age is the ultimate irrationality of our civilization:
War. In the face of that challenge the cocky optimism of
the logical positivists, for instance, may well seem less com-
pelling than the elaborate despair of the existentialists.

Christian Science itself has had to face the test of two
world wars in this century and has found itself strengthened
by the experience. Christian Scientists have put their religion to work in army camps and on battlefields, in flaming

cockpits and muddy foxholes, on life rafts adrift in icy northern seas, in prison camps, in slave labor battalions, on death marches, in every sort of privation and terror and desperate boredom and violent uprooting. What emerged from these experiences was a great saga of healing, a remarkable witness to the sustaining and liberating power of Love.

The quality of the testimony meetings held by service men in base camps and outposts across the globe in World War II is not likely to be forgotten by any who experienced them. In Germany, where Christian Science was banned and went underground, and across the world in Japan, in Java, in Hong Kong, in the Philippines, many Christian Scientists —whether they belonged to the conquerors or the conquered —emerged from the ordeal with experiences that recalled Daniel in the lions' den or Paul and Silas in the inner prison at midnight.[15]

This is too large a story to be told in the present context. It sets the background, however, for any consideration of the Christian Science attitude to war. It invites the careful examination of any interested person who has casually assumed that Christian Science "ignores" evil and cures only "imaginary" ills. Clearly some Christian Scientists, at least, have faced evils of greater magnitude than many of their critics have experienced.

Thanks to UNESCO, it has become a platitude that "wars begin in the minds of men." Christian Science opposes to this the fact of one divine Mind in which are none of the destructive elements that constitute war. Interestingly enough, The Mother Church does not take a pacifist position, any more than it takes a chauvinistic or bellicose one, but leaves

---

[15] A small part of this is recorded in *The Story of Christian Science Wartime Activities, 1939–1946* (Boston, The Christian Science Publishing Society, 1947), and a good deal more in the testimony columns of the Christian Science periodicals during and subsequent to the war years.

the Christian Scientist free to work out the problem according to his highest spiritual understanding. In World War II a mere handful of Christian Scientists registered as pacifists; the vast majority of those called on to fight did so willingly and often with outstanding courage. But many a Christian Scientist went into the armed services holding firmly to the spiritual conviction that as an individual expression of the one divine Mind he could not bring death or harm to anyone; and a number of testimonies have told of men being placed in positions where they were able to do wholly constructive and healing work in the very midst of the death-dealing and destructive phases of war.

Each individual demonstration, however small, of victory over these destructive phases is considered by Christian Scientists to be an undermining of the whole gigantic fabric. Yet even if the individual Christian Scientist could eliminate them wholly from his experience by eliminating them scientifically from his thinking, the problem of war as an element in national policy would still remain. *The Christian Science Monitor*, for instance, must necessarily face the question of supporting national and international policies which inevitably, at this stage of human development, involve the maintaining and possible use of force. A valuable hint is found in Mrs. Eddy's last statement on the subject, made in 1908:

> For many years I have prayed daily that there be no more war, no more barbarous slaughtering of our fellow-beings; prayed that all the peoples on earth and the islands of the sea have one God, one Mind; love God supremely, and love their neighbor as themselves.
>
> National disagreements can be, and should be, arbitrated wisely, fairly; and fully settled.
>
> It is unquestionable, however, that at this hour the armament

of navies is necessary, for the purpose of preventing war and preserving peace among nations.

In line with this statement, the *Monitor* accepts the concept of armed force as a relative measure to restrain aggression, a measure fitted to the present moral immaturity of society as a whole. It looks in the direction of bringing military power under the restraints of a "police" purpose as part of a workable collective security system. In the present crisis it has supported the building up of western defensive strength as a counterpoise to Soviet power, while constantly urging in concrete ways that betterment of the West's moral, economic, political, and social outlook which alone can give it victory in the struggle for men's minds.

This may be made clearer by quoting an editorial from the *Monitor*, one of the rare ones that refers explicitly to the teachings of the paper's founder. It is always a little unfair to pluck out and exhibit out of context a journalistic statement written for a particular moment and meant to be considered in the daily flow of news and comment, some of which may have modified, amplified, and explained certain points left obscure or undeveloped in the particular passing utterance. This editorial appeared on November 28, 1951, during the Korean War, when American public opinion was being pushed dangerously in the direction of more drastic (and more impulsive) action:

> Millions of people are asking: What is the United States trying to do? Does its policy rest on the limited aim of containing Soviet power within its present bounds? Or does it rest on the unlimited aim of wiping police-state communism from the earth?
>
> Those who see the world crisis today as a problem in achieving a balance between two giant centers of power are fearful that American impetuosity, by reason of choosing the unlimited goal, may plunge the world into ruinous total war.

Those who believe, with the boundless ardor of the crusader, that this world cannot permanently endure half slave and half free fear only that traditional balance-of-power diplomacy, with compromise as the best it can hope for, may leave the real source of world enslavement untouched.

In general, it may be said that Europeans incline toward the limited goal. With their long experience in diplomacy, their practice in accommodating themselves to unhappy circumstance and human limitation, they can conceive of resisting further encroachments of Soviet power, but are deeply skeptical of a "holy war" carried to the heart of world communism.

In general, Americans tend to feel that sooner or later either democracy or communism must achieve a total and conclusive victory over the other. The moral idealism of Americans, as well as their exuberant energies and impatience for quick results, does not incline them favorably to half measures. At the same time it makes them more alert than many Europeans to the dynamism of the Communist challenge—which is like their own dynamic faith in reverse, not used to thinking in restricted terms.

Must the free world choose between these two goals: limited defense or unlimited victory? Has America nothing to learn from Europe's greater experience? Has Europe nothing to learn from America's greater expectancy?

The answer to all these questions is clear. The two points of view are complementary. It is a question of realizing which means should be directed toward limited ends, which toward unlimited ends. And this is no more than recognizing the difference between material and moral power. For while material power must always be limited and thus address itself to limited ends, moral or spiritual power is unlimited in scope and cannot properly stop short of perfect victory.

Thus the grand strategy of enlightened Christian thinking must always aim at the total elimination of all evil from human experience. But in the concrete situations with which military power and political diplomacy deal the ends must be carefully limited by the available resources of military and political strength—and to the specific purposes which such forms of power can serve.

The atom bomb may be an invaluable element in the free world's defense at the present time, but it can never wipe out communism's bid for men's minds. A needless blunder into atomic war could even increase the sum of totalitarian tyranny in the world by increasing the misery and despair on which such tyranny feeds. Material power may be called to the defense of enlightened thinking, but its aid must always be limited. When it dominates thinking, when offensive aims take control of defensive arms, tyranny has already crept in by the back door. Ultimately ideas must win and hold men to the side of freedom.

And here the boundless moral idealism of America (which Europeans sometimes see as mere naïveté) brings a breath of fresh hope to the world. For Americans are magnificently right in believing in the possibility of a completely free world. But the "holy war" for such a world must be fought with ideas—ideas not as intellectual abstractions but warm, living, clothed in good deeds, bringing help and healing and practical encouragement to a suffering world.

The Marshall Plan, the Point Four program, the goal of disarmament under world law, the concrete sense of universal brotherhood—here are a few elements in the only valid "holy war" against communism. Let there be no limits to the faith that inspires such actions and ideals. Let it be remembered that prayer can reach where propaganda cannot penetrate. Let the spirit and example of free men kindle fires of freedom all over the world.

And let us remember what the founder of this newspaper, Mary Baker Eddy, pointed out when she wrote in regard to the American Civil War: "A few immortal sentences, breathing the omnipotence of divine justice, have been potent to break despotic fetters and abolish the whipping-post and slave market; but oppression neither went down in blood, nor did the breath of freedom come from the cannon's mouth. Love is the liberator."

The generalizations in the next to the last paragraph obviously need further examples to define them with sufficient weight and precision. This is a case of journalistic shorthand, where ringing phrases must be given concrete content by subsequent analysis and application. One might say that the *Monitor*'s socio-political judgments in actual situations over a period of years furnish the only satisfactory "operational" definition of what it means by, for instance, "the spirit and example of free men."

Yet that is not the whole of it, either. Even the most enlightened views of trade, industry, diplomacy, civil liberties, race relations and so forth will never of themselves "kindle fires of freedom all over the world." In a revolutionary age only a revolutionary spiritual force can seize men's hearts, though paradoxically its effect may be to bring increasing reasonableness and moderation into the social process.

4.

Today the hydrogen bomb seems a kind of blasphemous parody on the words of Jesus: "If ye have faith as a grain of mustard seed, ye shall say unto this mountain, Remove hence to yonder place; and it shall remove: and nothing shall be impossible unto you." Where is the faith in Spirit equal to this challenge? Where is the understanding sufficient to harness the incalculable and life-giving forces of spiritual law?

The faith that has rocked the world with atomic explosions is a faith in man's capacity to control nature through scientific method, but today one often finds it coupled with a fearful doubt of man's ability to control himself. Christian faith may come to the rescue in this dilemma, but in its usual forms it is far removed from the blazing assurance and

unlimited claims of primitive Christianity. It is the conviction of Christian Scientists, as I have already noted, that Mrs.
Eddy's discovery has made available a spiritual power that
as greatly exceeds the usual forms of Christian influence as
atomic energy exceeds all prior forms of physical power.

This may well seem a preposterous claim to the world at
large, and Christian Scientists do well not to press it beyond
their present demonstration. Yet even a single instantaneous
healing of an organic disease at a supposedly incurable stage
challenges the basic concept of man as a pinpoint of dust
in astronomical space, subject to all the ruthless restrictions
of those provisional hypotheses which we commonly call
laws of nature. The implications for the thinker who has the
audacity to follow through the logic of such a healing may
be staggering.

Geoffrey Hoyland, whose analogy between the scientific
discovery of magnetism and that of a spiritual power beyond
our present measurement has already been quoted, writes
a further passage that is pertinent here. He reminds us that
magnetism appeared to the Victorian scientists as a force of
strictly limited range and capability. That brilliant pioneer
Faraday would probably have thought it quite impossible
that a five-ton steel armor plate should ever be lifted by
means of a magnet:

> There are some patterns in Nature, which though they can
> do a little, appear to be incapable of doing much—it is a case
> of "thus far and no farther." But Faraday would have been
> wrong, none the less; for a modern magnetic crane in a steel
> works can lift fantastic weights. Methods have been developed
> of concentrating the magnetic field to an extent which would
> have been regarded as impossible fifty years ago. *It is danger-
> ous, and unscientific, to say of any of the patterns of Nature
> that they must always be too weak, or too faint, to achieve a
> certain specified result.* Patterns have a disconcerting habit of

suddenly asserting themselves masterfully; the faint footpath over the heath changes overnight into an arterial road.

It is probable that many Christian Scientists fail to recognize the implications and possibilities of Christian Science in every field of thought and action. Consequently it is not surprising that even those outside commentators who grant a certain value to it are apt to see it as operating within rather narrow limits. A characteristic utterance here is that of James' onetime Harvard colleague, George Santayana, in his *Character and Opinion in the United States* (New York, Charles Scribner's Sons, 1920), p. 188 ff.:

To be poor in order to be simple, to produce less in order that the product may be more choice and beautiful, and may leave us less burdened with unnecessary duties and useless possessions—that is an ideal not articulate in the American mind; yet here and there I seem to have heard a sigh after it, a groan at the perpetual incubus of business and shrill society. Significant witness to such aspirations is borne by those new forms of popular religion, not mere variations on tradition, which have sprung up from the soil—revivalism, spiritualism, Christian Science, the New Thought. Whether or no we can tap, through these or other channels, some cosmic or other energy not hitherto at the disposal of man (and there is nothing incredible in that), we certainly may try to remove friction and waste in the mere process of living; we may relax morbid strains, lessen suppressed instincts, iron out the creases of the soul, discipline ourselves into simplicity, sweetness, and peace. These religious movements are efforts toward such physiological economy and hygiene; and while they are thoroughly plebeian, with no great lights, and no idea of raising men from the most vulgar and humdrum worldly existence, yet they see the possibility of physical and moral health on that common plane, and pursue it. That is true morality.

Christian Scientists would of course demur at the lack of discrimination that links them casually with spiritualism and New Thought, but their objection to this derives its real force from Santayana's assumption that Christian Science, like these others, has "no idea of raising men from the most vulgar and humdrum worldly existence." While it is true that some Christian Scientists may seem to equate the good life with the conventional American ideal of business and social success, observation indicates that as their understanding of Christian Science deepens it not only brings a higher degree of "simplicity, sweetness, and peace" into their lives but eventually tends to open their minds and hearts to ideals completely outside the pattern they have hitherto followed. Sometimes the transformation of values is sudden and spectacular; more often it is gradual and uneven. While Mrs. Eddy herself constantly stressed the revolutionary nature of Christian Science, she said to those who might be inclined to be overzealous or fanatical: "Emerge gently from matter into Spirit."

In a talk given over the Third Programme of the British Broadcasting Corporation in 1953 the process was put in this way:

When one throws a stone into a pond, it starts a ripple flowing out from the center of disturbance in a constantly widening series of concentric circles. So when an individual first tries to understand and practice Christian Science, it begins at once to revolutionize his thinking, first of all about those things closest to him and then gradually about a widening circle of concerns. In a rather literal sense his body is that which is closest to him, and he begins to exercise dominion over it with the authority of his newly recognized spiritual selfhood. Then he finds much in his human character and temperament that must be transformed, and much in his personal relations, his business, his profession, the world of affairs, and the world of intellect.

The Christian Science Monitor is already touching the world of affairs; it is noteworthy that the paper's brilliant editor, Erwin D. Canham, in various writings and speeches has also been exploring some of the revolutionary changes in the world of intellect which may be linked with the metaphysical insights of Christian Science. These changes are most apparent in the natural sciences and in relation to the basic concept of matter.

The opening sentence of Mrs. Eddy's "scientific statement of being" reads: "There is no life, truth, intelligence, nor substance in matter." To the natural scientist of her own day the statement was sheer nonsense. But any physicist today could accept it with perfect ease—even though he would mean by it something different from what she meant and might be a long way from accepting the sentence that follows it: "All is infinite Mind and its infinite manifestation, for God is All-in-all." The indestructible matter-stuff of classical Newtonian physics has been blasted sky-high, and the energy into which it is convertible is far more readily recognizable as a form of consciousness today than when Mrs. Eddy wrote boldly: "Physical force and mortal mind are one."

Christian Scientists who are physicists are for the most part very cautious about throwing theoretical bridges between the two disciplines. They recognize that the *direction* of modern physics is diminishing the gap between natural science and Christian Science, but they realize the vast distance there still is to go before scientific theory and Christian Science demonstration approach the point where matter is seen to be an impossible limit on spiritual force.

Nevertheless, since every healing of organic disease by spiritual means involves bodily changes unpredictable on the basis of physical as well as chemical and physiological laws, it is clear to them that eventually Christian Science must challenge natural science at every point. Thus they are able to accept even the most far-reaching prophecies of Mrs. Eddy, as when she writes:

> The elements and functions of the physical body and of the physical world will change as mortal mind changes its beliefs. . . . The seasons will come and go with changes of time and tide, cold and heat, latitude and longitude. The agriculturist will find that these changes cannot affect his crops. "As a vesture shalt Thou change them and they shall be changed." The mariner will have dominion over the atmosphere and the great deep, over the fish of the sea and the fowls of the air. The astronomer will no longer look up to the stars,—he will look out from them upon the universe; and the florist will find his flower before its seed.

In a certain sense, parts of this prophecy have already been fulfilled. It is interesting that there are Christian Scientists today doing advanced experimental work in plant physiology, agricultural biochemistry, and similar fields—I speak only of those of whom I have personal knowledge—as well as in meteorology, rocket research, and astronomy. There are farmers, too, who have had striking instances of the prevention or healing of blight, pest, crop failures resulting from weather conditions, hoof-and-mouth disease, and similar farm problems through Christian Science. Some of these experiences have found their way as testimonies into the Christian Science periodicals, but some of the best of them have not—for most Christian Scientists feel that it is a mistake to challenge the credulity of the age too sharply.

It is obvious that the frontiers of Christian Science demonstration can and must be pushed in all directions if its ultimate claims are to be validated. But here again Mrs. Eddy's advice to "emerge gently" is apposite. In *Science and Health* she makes it clear that Christian Scientists are expected to eat and drink normally at this stage of human existence; in a similar manner they enjoy the fruits of modern scientific and technological advance—and even participate actively in that advance—without feeling the need of challenging its present methods beyond their own ability to demonstrate, and the world's readiness to tolerate, such a challenge.

"We welcome the increase of knowledge and the end of error," wrote Mrs. Eddy, "because even human invention must have its day, and we want that day to be succeeded by Christian Science, by divine reality." In this respect she faced wholly toward the twentieth century. When an interviewer for the New York *Herald* asked her in 1901 what she thought of "modern material inventions," she replied: "Oh, we cannot oppose them. . . . We use them, we make them our figures of speech. They are preparing the way for us." Her own high respect for academic education and technical research, as well as the solid achievements of Christian Scientists in various fields of study since her day, removes any taint of obscurantism from Christain Science. "Observation, invention, study, and original thought are expansive," she wrote, "and should promote the growth of mortal mind out of itself, out of all that is mortal."

Thus a Christian Scientist may work within any of the intellectual disciplines or the arts without feeling any sharp clash of interest with his religious convictions. In fact, the latter may enable him to pursue his work with considerably greater effectiveness. I have known musicians, architects, sociologists, biologists, mathematicians, who have found that Christian Science has enabled them to work out difficult problems in their fields in what sometimes seemed startling ways. They would explain this as a surrendering of the human mind to the divine Mind and a consequent banishing of the fear, the bias, the self-importance, or any of the manifold other factors that might stand in the way of the problem's solution. As they advance in Christian Science, however, they sometimes find that they are applying it not only to the manner but to the matter of their work, finding radically new creative insights into their subjects. This is the point where both caution and high expectancy are in order. This is the point of revolutionary challenge, where Christian Science will eventually have to prove itself as it already has on the level of bodily healing and moral regeneration.

Predictions are rash at this point. The achievements of Christian Science must define its own potentialities. Poetry may prophesy, but scientific demonstration is something else again. One remembers the words Emerson put into the mouth of his "Orphic poet," Bronson Alcott, in *Nature:*

> Build therefore your own world. As fast as you conform your life to the pure idea in your mind, that will unfold its great proportions. . . . As when the summer comes from the south the snow-banks melt and the face of the earth becomes green before it, so shall the advancing spirit create its orna- ments along its path, and carry with it the beauty it visits and the song which enchants it; it shall draw beautiful faces, warm hearts, wise discourse, and heroic acts, around its way, until evil is no more seen. The kingdom of man over nature, which cometh not with observation,—a dominion such as now is be- yond his dream of God,—he shall enter without more wonder than the blind man feels who is gradually restored to perfect sight.

This is fine, but it is poetry. Christian Science would trans- late it, step by step, into fact. The essential language of Christian Science is deeds rather than words. At the same time it is a question whether Christian Science will ever have an explicit, recognizable aesthetic expression of its own—a distinctive poetry, for instance, to match its vision fully. Only the event can answer this question. There are and will be Christian Scientists who are artists, perhaps great artists, and Christian Science should normally lead to a deeper appreciation of the arts than is usual in a mass-production society. But the fullest expression of the art of Christian Science must always be in living, in *being* as a whole, though this will include the emancipation of the individual into a larger measure of freedom in any activity in which he engages, including the arts. A Christian Science practitioner, Mary Burt Messer, who has written some arresting poetry, suggests something of this in a brief lyric in which she asks:

> Is it more than lyric can
> To etch the magnitude of man—
> Man within whose stretch of bloom
> Arc of universe finds room
> From the star-sprent Milky Way
> To the dire, the lovely day?
> How at once irradiant
> And with doom so darkly blent?
> Rainbow-tinted . . . crashed and spent?
>
> Why, this is the stuff of dreams:
> Phantom rafters, beam on beam,
> Nothing is the thing it seems.
>
> Pierce with lance of seeing eye
> Soundlessly it passes by.
> Whence with rapt surprise will break
> Man sublime and stark awake.

Again, in an unpublished manuscript (a work in progress) from which I am permitted to quote, a Christian Scientist writes of the experience of healing:

What is appearing is a waking up to immortality. . . . This realization is beyond the mere advantage, in its practical aspects, of any cure, however precious that may be. For healing, much more than a needed rescue, is a mode of speech. Spiritual meanings, in their altogether-loveliness, are hard things to tell. The human mind cleaves to material reality, as it conceives it—

or misconceives it; losing its way as to the things of Spirit, except as these relate somehow to the familiar and the known.

Christ Jesus preached little—at least in proportion to his acts. He had another mode of reaching human consciousness. The speech of Jesus which marked his ministry and distinguished it from all others before it was his miracles—as they seemed to those about him. The human mind was thus reached by the touch of healing.

"The Word was made flesh, and dwelt among us . . . full of grace and truth."

Contrast this with the method of philosophy, its dialectic, its detachment from the human need. Set philosophy beside the actual healing of the palsied man, the blind, the lame. The infinite breaks into a new kind of utterance, speaking the language comprehensible to men.

Here is an approach to what might be called the semantics of Christian Science. Mrs. Eddy frequently deplored the inadequacy of language to convey her meaning. In time she worked out a basic vocabulary which, together with her system of capitalization, is very exact for its purpose, however chaotic it may look to the superficial observer. But she remained suspicious of all *verbal* religion. "The error of the ages," she wrote, "is preaching without practice." Even audible prayer seemed to her to run the danger of reaching beyond the speaker's real desires, so she banished it, except for the Lord's Prayer, from her services, and substituted silent prayer instead. On this subject she wrote, with a characteristically practical emphasis: "True prayer is not asking God for love; it is learning to love, and to include all mankind in one affection. Prayer is the utilization of the love wherewith He loves us."

Probably the semantic barrier is one of the chief obstacles to a wider understanding of Christian Science. We live in an age that distrusts large abstractions. The great metaphysical structures of Aquinas and Hegel have gone down before the semantic demolition squad. To the logical positivist or operationalist the statement, "God is Love," is completely meaningless. But the healing that follows from a conviction that God *is* Love is a fact to be reckoned with.

In his pioneer study, *Christian Science and Philosophy*, Steiger quotes the promise of Jesus that he will send the Comforter or "Spirit of truth" to teach his disciples "all things," and suggests the identification of this Comforter as "an ethico-metaphysical science." Pointing out the unique relationship of experience to metaphysics in Christian Science, he draws a vital distinction which corresponds to that of Mrs. Eddy's statement, "Infinite progression is concrete being, which finite mortals see and comprehend only as abstract glory," and indicates the gulf between operative Christian Science and all forms of transcendental abstraction:

To the formalist metaphysics is a limit, an absolute, the concept of the unconceptual. But this does not prevent metaphysics from having a normative function for the human consciousness and an attraction which makes metaphysics appear to be the highest conceivable value. Metaphysics is, therefore, not only a totality, unity or oneness, but is man's supreme value, and all teleology can be explained as an urge for a full realization of that supreme value. It can be assumed that human consciousness, liberated from the images of mortal mind, may be capable of the full experience of a metaphysical universe, of which the mortal mind concept was only a misrepresentation. Metaphysics is abstract only to an erroneous point of view, and liberation from this wrong point of view may bring experiences incommensurable with conceptual thought.

In this connection Kant's warning against undue speculation about a spiritual universe should not be overlooked. Conceptual thought has its limitations and must content itself with the transcendental aspects of metaphysics which consist in a realization of metaphysical value. The full realization of the supreme value is salvation from a wrong concept of existence.

Mrs. Eddy makes the same point when she writes: "Science is not susceptible of being held as a mere theory." This is where her insistence on operational definitions is all-important. Take, for instance, her formal definition of God as "the all-knowing, all-seeing, all-acting, all-wise, all-loving, and eternal; Principle; Mind; Soul; Spirit; Life; Truth; Love." This has meaning only as it is *acted from* or defined by experience. Thus she writes elsewhere: "As Christian Scientists you seek to define God to your own consciousness by feeling and applying the nature and practical possibilities of divine Love." But the same might be said of each of the other synonyms of Deity; in one sense a Christian Scientist's whole life, in so far as he is practicing Christian Science, is an endeavor to define these seven synonyms to himself more adequately in terms of experience.

In this effort he looks to the perfect example of Jesus, of whom Mrs. Eddy wrote: "Out of the amplitude of his pure affection, he defined Love." When Pilate asked Jesus, "What is truth?" the Nazarene did not answer him with words; his whole life was the answer—not the least of it being the supreme definition of Life he was about to give through the Resurrection. Here, in fact, was the perfect definition of man in God's image, which otherwise would have remained an abstract ideal without relevance to concrete human experience. Yet to him the ideal *was* the concrete. The Word was made flesh, but it was the Word that was eternally real; speaking absolutely, Jesus himself could say that "the flesh profiteth *nothing*."

Thus all questions of historicity in connection with his life, as Mrs. Eddy once pointed out to the skeptical and argumentative Wiggin,[16] were secondary to the revelation of the ideal man through the Christ in individual consciousness. That long agony of scholarship which Schweitzer sums up as *The Quest of the Historical Jesus* is to be resolved by the concrete demonstration of the Christ in healing, by the modern reproduction of those marvels which the higher critics have considered as invalidating the Bible record wherever they occur. Science, instead of destroying the basis of faith, will then support it, and the expanding demonstration of the modern disciple will help to explain Mrs. Eddy's arresting statement: "Jesus of Nazareth was the most scientific man that ever trod the globe."

Christian Scientists have reason to be modest about their present demonstration of the vast Principle they profess. They have a long way to go in translating the spiritual potential of their religion into concrete accomplishments at every level of human experience and in every field of thought and endeavor. That they have gone some distance is proved by the record. Even certain acidulous critics have borne witness to that fact. Dr. Leslie Weatherhead, in his book *Psychology, Religion and Healing*, gives a scathing picture of Christian Science as he understands it, accepts uncritically numerous calumnies against Mrs. Eddy, repeats unwittingly various time-worn misrepresentations of her teachings, but adds with a frank honesty that springs from the fundamental integrity of his purpose:

---

16 *The First Church of Christ, Scientist, and Miscellany*, p. 318 f. This statement has sometimes been wrested from its context to imply that Mrs. Eddy considered the lifework of Jesus Christ as "unnecessary." Seen in perspective, it is no more susceptible of such an interpretation than is the statement of the evangelist Billy Graham that even if "there were no historical record of Jesus' life and ministry, He would still be real to me because I know Him by personal and daily experience." Cf. Kierkegaard: "There is no disciple at second hand. . . . For whoever has what he has from God himself clearly has it at first hand; and he who does not have it from God himself is not a disciple."

While we may criticise many things in Christian Science, I must pay tribute here to the characters of Christian Scientists. Those I have met have not seemed proud or intolerant. They have seemed to me humble, inwardly serene and radiant, and to be in touch with spiritual resources which are all too commonly untapped. Their conception of the reality and power of God is finer than most, and rids their minds of fear. In the main they seem healthy, loving and forgiving people, practised in the discipline of excluding from themselves "hatred, malice and all uncharitableness." Above all they appear to me really to love others in the Christian sense and I am more and more convinced of the therapeutic energies released by such loving.

So far, so good. But divine Love, by definition, is without limits. Its therapeutic energies must be at least equal to any conceivable combination of physical forces, to any imaginable challenge of earthly wretchedness, to any possible enrichment of human values. The Christian Scientist who stands dazzled before the implications opened to him by the healing power of Love as he has experienced it may long impatiently for Christian Scientists to push more boldly into broader areas of thought and action—areas which have not yet felt the transforming power of this new understanding of the Christ. But if he grows discouraged by the magnitude of the task or the slowness of the progress, he will do well to remember Mrs. Eddy's wise words in *Science and Health*: "Judge not the future advancement of Christian Science by the steps already taken, lest you yourself be condemned for failing to take the first step."

CONCLUSION

And I saw another mighty angel come down from heaven, clothed with a cloud; and a rainbow was upon his head, and his face was as it were the sun, and his feet as pillars of fire; and he had in his hand a little book open. . . . And the voice which I heard from heaven spake unto me again, and said, Go and take the little book which is open in the hand of the angel which standeth upon the sea and upon the earth. And I went unto the angel, and said unto him, Give me the little book. And he said unto me, Take it, and eat it up; and it shall make thy belly bitter, but it shall be in thy mouth sweet as honey.

The Revelation of Saint John

Mortals, obey the heavenly evangel. Take divine Science. Read this book from beginning to end. Study it, ponder it. It will be indeed sweet at its first taste, when it heals you; but murmur not over Truth, if you find its digestion bitter.

Science and Health with
Key to the Scriptures

AMERICA WAS BORN IN OPTIMISM. Transcendentalism carried optimism to the pitch of poetry, to a visionary level at which it seemed not impossible that the kingdom of heaven should descend at last to New England. Pragmatism substituted a technological utopia for the heavenly kingdom and found in the new instrumentality of scientific method the justification for a still ebullient hope. But America at mid-century finds itself possessed of a strange disquiet; despite all its ardent and even strident affirmations, a dark doubt stirs in its collective thinking.

It is partly a matter of growing up. Americans have discovered that they are involved after all in the common fate

197

of mankind. They find themselves compelled to consider the problems of other and older peoples for whom life has been a tragic burden rather than an open opportunity. Their own traditional optimism begins to look more like the natural high spirits of youth than the rounded wisdom of maturity. The gadget civilization of which they are so proud has laid a time-bomb in the powerhouse; and mystery, banished with the wilderness, stares back at them from their own bewildered hearts.

The situation has been well analyzed in one of the representative American books of this period, Russell W. Davenport's *The Dignity of Man* (New York, Harper & Brothers, 1955). Deeply dissatisfied with an optimism that refuses to recognize the natural limits on human power, Davenport realized that the optimistic tradition is too deeply woven into American life to be abandoned entirely without abandoning America itself. Yet does that mean that the deep "pessimistic" insights of the great saints and seers must therefore be excluded—those insights into mortality which rebuke the bustling pride of finite man, forever intent on building new Babels to heaven? Davenport writes:

> May there not be some means by which these two conflicting views of man can be reconciled? To put the question more specifically, may it not be that that inward-looking view of reality which characterizes the pursuit of happiness of the Buddhist monk, and which leads to such pessimistic conclusions regarding life on earth, is in some valid way connected with the outward-looking view, which so deeply influences American life and leads to such optimistic evaluations? Is it really the case that one of these views of human life is true, and the other false, and that the human being, therefore, must choose between them? May it not be true that each represents a different aspect of the human struggle, that one supports the other, that one can be fulfilled in terms of the other? May there

not be available to him who is willing to seek for it, a mighty synthesis between the great hopes that Americans have for mankind, and the old and wiser sense of tragedy that has for so many centuries filled the hearts of seers—a synthesis which, could we discover it, might provide us with the foundations for a doctrine of freedom possessing that quality which our present foundations so glaringly lack, the quality of universality?

Davenport himself came close to the heart of the problem in his recognition of the fallibility of all hopes based on man as matter—that matter whose ultimate unreality he almost glimpsed but which struck him down in death before his book was finished. His deeply searching spirit symbolizes the distrust of thinking Americans today in the easy solutions promised by yesterday's optimism. The "power of positive thinking," as popularly practiced, may suffice to buoy a man up as he faces his daily trials, but it can hardly satisfy the individual who confronts unflinchingly the whole dark range of evil in mortal existence. For cruelty and indifference to man's highest aspirations are inherent in the very texture of the material universe; so long as man is defined as matter he is implicated in an essentially amoral natural order.

Here is the hard fact from which Transcendentalism averted its gaze. Even an Alcott failed to heed the New Testament warning that flesh and blood cannot inherit the kingdom of God nor can corruption inherit incorruption. He looked for perfection in human beings and in human society, and he obviously failed to find it. Alcott is one of the saints of American life, but he is also one of its most illuminating failures, for his idealism only translated into transcendental terms the common assumptions of American society.

In revolt against the discredited perfectionism of a more naïve age, many Americans today have turned to Reinhold Niebuhr's ironic insights into the essential fallibility of human nature; yet in this neo-orthodox emphasis on man as tragically fallen away from God, they have surrendered the crystalline freshness of the primitive Christian message, with its ringing command: "Be ye therefore perfect, even as your Father which is in heaven is perfect." They have learned more about the sort of world they are living in, but have lost the vision of that unsullied Principle of perfection which Jesus presented to man as a loving Father, of whom he could say: "Fear not, little flock; for it is your Father's good pleasure to give you the kingdom"—the present consciousness of spiritual perfection.

It is for this reason that Niebuhr's thought—for all its valuable contributions to American intellectual maturity, for all its political energy and social fruitfulness—belongs more to Europe than to an America where faith in a limitless good still fights for existence. This gives significance to a statement by a European observer of America published in the very year of the stock market crash which struck one of the first great blows at America's easy optimism. Count Hermann Keyserling, now almost forgotten by Americans but still remembered with interest by Europeans, wrote at that time in his *America Set Free* (New York, Harper & Brothers, 1929):

> Now the law of compensation is best exemplified by Christian Science, the prototype of American religiousness; and the example of this religion, again, provides the best proof imaginable—for such as want proofs—of the reality underlying its idea. *If* matter is overemphasized in the United States, and *if* there is such a thing as spiritual reality, then it follows *a priori*, from the general knowledge we have of the human soul, that spirituality in America should differentiate with equal onesidedness. So it actually does; the quality of "purity" determined by Puritanism, in its turn, adds to the clearness of the contours. Further: *if* the fundamental attitude in the United

States is one of spiritual passivity, then some attitude which is all the more pronounced in its activity must needs compensate it in the general system. This is precisely the meaning of the uncompromising affirmations and denials of Christian Science. Within a nation individuals play the same part as do particular functions within the individual soul. We thus find that every spiritual American who can be considered as representative, actually belongs, whether he knows it or not, to the wider circle of Christian Science. It would perhaps be more correct, from the point of view of fact, to say that somehow or other he belongs to New Thought. Emerson, for instance, undoubtedly did, whereas one could not have called him a Christian Scientist. But on the plane of significance, Christian Science and no other expression of American religiousness stands out as the prototype—no matter whether New Thought may have preceded it in time—because it best conforms to the law of correlation between meaning and expression. At this point, some may object that the primitivity of the notions of Christian Science makes them unfit to express truth in any way. But this objection is not valid. . . .

Every quality of life expresses itself in two opposite ways, actively and passively, as Ethos and as Pathos. In the form of Ethos, American Christianity corresponds exactly to the Russian as the representative of Pathos. Here, then we find one more example of the laws of correlation and compensation. On many previous occasions we have come to the conclusion that materialist America and Bolshevik Russia are closely akin in spirit. But for that very reason spiritual America and early Christian Russia are as closely related. Europe often regards Russian religiosity with awe, even expecting it to be the salvation of the world. But then it ought to assume the same attitude toward American spirituality. Of this one hears little. Yet the great successes Christian Science can boast of even on European soil are due to a psychological situation which is primarily identical with that of Russia. Christian Science is as far removed from a normal European religion as Russian Christianity is. But it is as representative of pure spirituality. If, accordingly, an intellectual and oversophisticated European feels that his salvation lies in the direction of primitivity, he will find it in America as well as in Russia, his choice depending on whether his soul is more of an active or a passive quality.

Though some of Keyserling's generalizations are questionable, there are several very good discriminations here, particularly in the line drawn between Christian Science and New Thought, a distinction which supports the thesis developed in the present book. The passage takes us into questions beyond the scope of this book, but it suggests some valuable lines of exploration. To be sure, it is important that Christian Science be understood as more than a phenomenon of American culture, but Keyserling recognizes in a degree that it possesses that quality of universality which Davenport felt American optimism so eminently lacked. Christian Scientists may bridle at the word "primitivity" as applied to their religion (though they themselves speak of it as a restoration of *primitive* Christianity), but they will be less disturbed if they think of the word as indicating an unsophisticated expression of natural spirituality. Mrs. Eddy herself repudiated the idea that all revelation must come "from the schools and along the line of scholarly and ecclesiastical descent, as kings are crowned from a royal dynasty."

What is most suggestive here, however, is the concept of Christian Science as a sort of spiritual ultimate, so far at least as active spirituality is concerned. For beyond all the careful calculations of scientific credibility and pragmatic usefulness, our sense of fitness demands that the highest spiritual values shall have a quality of *daring*, a total commitment to God regardless of what may be the practical result. Luther expressed it in his demand for a "daring, reckless confidence in the grace of God." Job said with stark simplicity: "Though he slay me, yet will I trust in him."

This is the spirit of Christian Science at its point of departure from the world of the senses. It leaves all for God, all the lesser comforts, all the easy compromises. If a man's spiritual understanding prove unequal to the physical challenge that confronts him, then he may choose to suffer what appears to the world as defeat rather than doubt the omnipotence of Love or its willingness to heal him. If his courage fail, he may yet summon up new spiritual strength from the depths of a conviction so wholly anchored in the divine that it has no taint of human pride or will or weakness. And in this very abandonment to the love of God, in this very acknowledgment of utter helplessness to be or do anything that He has not purposed, a man may find the revelation of a good beyond anything he has dared to hope. It is at the moment of total self-surrender that the fountaining joy at the heart of existence leaps forth as healing, as resurrection, as victory.

Mrs. Eddy never pretended that the heights of Christian Science were to be gained without a struggle. In her superb chapter on the Apocalypse in *Science and Health*—marked by deep flashes of poetry as she explores the symbolism of the angel clothed with a cloud, the woman clothed with the sun, and all those other tremendous metaphors—she portrays the dragon's war against the woman as type and shadow of the carnal mind's enmity against pure spirituality. "From Genesis to the Apocalypse, sin, sickness, and death, envy, hatred, and revenge,—all evil,—are typified by a serpent, or animal subtlety," she writes. "In the Apocalypse, when nearing its doom, this evil increases and becomes the great red dragon, swollen with sin, inflamed with war against spirituality, and ripe for destruction. It is full of lust and hate, loathing the brightness of divine glory." But before the Lamb of Love, before the innocence of the spiritual idea sacrificing all claim to selfhood apart from God, the dragon is cast down to earth—dust to dust, that dust which modern physics has already robbed of its ancient claim to substantiality and which Christian Science dismisses as nothingness, an impossible limit on the power of Love.

In Revelation 12:10, 11 we read the words: "And I heard a loud voice saying in heaven, Now is come salvation, and strength, and the kingdom of our God, and the power of his Christ: for the accuser of our brethren is cast down, which accused them before our God day and night. And they overcame him by the blood of the Lamb, and by the word of their testimony; and they loved not their lives unto the death."

Commenting on this, Mrs. Eddy writes, in words which gain in scope as one remembers that for her the word "sin" extended far beyond a narrow moralistic meaning to include the whole range of mortal error: "For victory over a single sin, we give thanks and magnify the Lord of Hosts. What shall we say of the mighty conquest over all sin? A louder song, sweeter than has ever before reached high heaven, now rises clearer and nearer to the great heart of Christ; for the accuser is not there, and Love sends forth her primal and everlasting strain."

APPENDIXES

Alcott's Theory of Education

(The following abridged version of Alcott's introduction to *Conversations with Children on the Gospels* (Boston, James Munroe & Co., 1836), is included because of its inaccessibility to most readers and its striking pertinence to the theme of the present book.)

Human Culture is the art of revealing to a man the true Idea of his Being—his endowments—his possessions—and of fitting him to use these for the growth, renewal, and perfection of his Spirit. It seeks to realize in the Soul the Image of the Creator.

This divine Art, including all others, or subordinating them to its Idea, was never apprehended, in all its breadth and depth of significance, till the era of Jesus of Nazareth. He it was that first revealed it. Over his Divine Intellect first flitted the Idea of man's endowments and destiny. He set no limits to the growth of our nature. "Be Ye Perfect even as my Father in Heaven is Perfect," was the high aim which he placed before his disciples; and in this he was true to our nature, for the sentiment lives in every faculty and function of our being. It is the ever-sounding Trump of Duty, urging us to the perpetual work of self-renewal. It is the deep instinct of the spirit. And his Life gives us the promise of its realization. In his attributes and endowments he is a Type of our common nature. His achievements are a glimpse of the Apotheosis of Humanity. They are a glorious unfolding of the Godlike in man. They disclose the Idea of Spirit. And if he was not, in himself, the complete fulfilment of Spirit, he apprehended its law, and set forth its conditions. He bequeathed to us the phenomena of its manifestation; for in the Gospels we have the history of Spirit accomplishing its mission on the earth. We behold the Incarnate One, dealing with flesh and blood—tempted, and suffering—yet baffling and overcoming the ministries of Evil and of Pain.

Still this Idea, so clearly announced, and so fully demonstrated in the being and life of Jesus, has made but little advance in the minds of men. It has been restricted to himself alone. Men do not deem him as the harmonious unfolding of Spirit into the Image of a Perfect Man—as a worthy Symbol of the Divinity, wherein Human Nature is revealed in its Fulness. Yet, as if by an inward and irresistible Instinct, all men have been drawn to him; and while diverse in their opinions, explaining his Idea in different types, they have given him the full and unreserved homage of their hearts.

It is the mission of this Age, to revive his Idea, give it currency, and reinstate it in the faith of men. By its quickening agency, it is to fructify our common nature, and reproduce its like. It is to unfold our being into the same divine likeness. The faded Image of Humanity is to be restored, and man reappear in his original brightness. It is to mould anew our Institutions, our Manners, our Men. The Divine Idea of a Man is to be formed in the common consciousness of this age, and genius mould all its products in accordance with it.

The means for reinstating this Idea in the common mind, in order to conduce to these results, are many. Yet all are simple. And the most direct and effectual are by apprehending the Genius of this Divine Man, from the study of those Records wherein his career is delineated with so much fidelity, simplicity, and truth. The Divine Idea of Humanity gleams forth through every circumstance of his terrestrial career. The Son of God appears on Earth, enrobed in Flesh, and looks forth serenely upon Man. We feel the significance of the Incarnation; the grandeur of our nature. We associate Jesus with our holiest aspirations, our deepest affections; and thus does he become a fit Mediator between the last age and the new era, of which he was the herald and the pledge. He is to us the Prophet of two millenniums. He is the brightest Symbol of a Man that history affords, and points us to yet fuller manifestations of the Godhead.

And the Gospels are not only a fit Text-Book for the study of

Spirit, in its corporeal relations, but they are a specimen also of the true method of imparting instruction. They give us the practice of Jesus himself. They unfold the means of addressing human nature. Jesus was a Teacher; he sought to renovate Humanity. His method commends itself to us. It is a beautiful exhibition of his Genius, bearing the stamp of naturalness, force, and directness. It is popular. Instead of seeking formal and austere means, he rested his influence chiefly on the living word, rising spontaneously in the soul, and clothing itself at once, in the simplest, yet most commanding forms. He was a finished extemporaneous speaker. Listen to him when seated at the well-side discoursing with the Samaritan woman, on the IDEA OF WORSHIP; and at night with Nicodemus, on SPIRITUAL RENEWAL. From facts and objects the most familiar, he slid easily into the highest and holiest themes, and, in this imposing guise, disclosed the great Doctrines, and stated the Divine Ideas, that it was his mission to bequeath to his race. Conversation was the form of utterance that he sought.

And Genius has ever sought this organ of utterance. Socrates—a name that Christians can see coupled with that of their Divine Sage—descanted thus on the profound themes in which he delighted. The market-place; the workshop; the public streets were his favorite haunts of instruction. And the divine Plato has added his testimony, also, in those enduring works, wherein he sought to embalm for posterity, both the wisdom of his master and the genius that was his own.

It is by such organs that Human Nature is to be unfolded into the Idea of its fulness. Yet to do this, teachers must be men in possession of their Idea. They must be men of their kind; men inspired with great and living Ideas, as was Jesus. And such are ever sent at the call of Humanity. Some God, instinct with the Idea that is to regenerate his era, is ever vouchsafed. As a flaming Herald he appears in his time, and sends abroad the Idea which it is the mission of the age to organize in institutions, and quicken into manners. Such mould the Genius of the time. They revive in Humanity the lost idea of its destiny, and reveal its fearful endowments. They vindicate the divinity of man's nature, and foreshadow on the coming Time the conquests that await it. An Age pre-exists in them; and History is but the manifestation and issue of their Wisdom and Will. They are the Prophets of the Future.

At this day, men need some revelation of Genius, to arouse them to a sense of their nature; for the Divine Idea of a Man seems to have died out of our consciousness. Encumbered by the gluts of the appetites, sunk in the corporeal senses, men know not the divine life that stirs within them, yet hidden and enchained. They revere not their own nature. And when the phenomenon of Genius appears, they marvel at its advent. They cannot own it. Laden with the gifts of the Divinity it touches their orb. At intervals of a century it appears. Some Nature, struggling with vicissitude, tempts forth the Idea of Spirit from within, and unlooses the Promethean God to roam free over the earth. He possesses his Idea and brings it as a blessed gift to his race. With awe-struck visage, the tribes of semi-unfolded beings survey it from below, deeming it a partial or preternatural gift of the Divinity, into whose life and being they are forbidden, by a decree of the Eternal, from entering; whose law they must obey, yet cannot apprehend. They dream not, that this phenomenon is but the complement of their common nature; and that in this admiration and obedience, which they proffer, is both the promise and pledge of the same powers in themselves; that this is but their fellow-creature in the flesh.

For Genius is but the free and harmonious play of all the faculties of a human being. It is a Man possessing his Idea and working with it. It is human nature rising superior to things and events, and transfiguring these into the image of its own Spiritual Ideal.

Yet among us Genius is at its wane. Human Nature appears shorn of her beams. We estimate man too low to hope for bright manifestations. And our views create the imperfection that mocks us. We have neither great men, nor good institutions.

To work worthily, man must aspire worthily. His theory of human attainment must be lofty. It must ever be lifting him above the low plain of custom and convention, in which the senses confine him, into the high mount of vision, and of renovating ideas.

To a divine nature, the sun ever rises over the mountains of hope, and brings promises on its wings. For Faith is the soul of all improvement. It is the Will of an Idea. It is an Idea seeking to embody and reproduce itself. It is the All-Proceeding Word going forth, as in the beginning of things, to incarnate itself, and become flesh and blood to the senses. Without this faith an Idea works no good. It is this which animates and quickens it into life. And this must come from living men.

And such Faith is the possession of all who apprehend Ideas. Such faith had Jesus, and this it was that empowered him to do the mighty works of which we read. It is this which inspired his genius. And Genius alone can inspire others. To nurse the young spirit as it puts forth its pinions in the fair and hopeful morning of life, it must be placed under the kindly and sympathising agency of Genius—heaven-inspired and hallowed—or there is no certainty that its aspirations will not die away in the routine of formal tuition, or spend themselves in the animal propensities that coexist with it. Teachers must be men of genius. They must be men inspired. The Divine Idea of a Man must have been unfolded from their being, and be a living presence. Philosophers, and Sages, and Seers,—the only real men—must come as of old, to the holy vocation of unfolding human nature. Socrates, and Plato, and the Diviner Jesus, must be raised up to us, to breathe their wisdom and will into the genius of our era, to recast our institutions, remould our manners, and regenerate our men. Philosophy and Religion, descending from the regions of cloudy speculation, must thus become denizens of our common earth, known among us as friends, and uttering their saving truths through the mouths of our little ones. Thus shall our being be unfolded. Thus the Idea of a man be reinstated in our consciousness.

To fulfil its end, Instruction must be an Inspiration. The true Teacher, like Jesus, must inspire in order to unfold. The Soul is touched by the live coal of his lips. A kindling influence goes forth to inspire; making the mind think; the heart feel; the pulse throb with his own. He arouses every faculty. He awakens the Godlike. He images the fair and full features of a Man. And thus doth he drive at will the drowsy Brute, that the Eternal hath yoked to the chariot of Life, to urge man across the Finite!

Our plans of influence, to be successful, must become more practical. We must be more faithful. We must deal less in abstractions; depend less on precepts and rules. Duty must sally forth an attending Presence into the work-day world, and organize to itself a living body. It must learn the art of uses. It must incorporate itself with Nature. To its sentiments we must give a Heart. Its Ideas we must arm with Hands. For it ever longs to become flesh and blood. The Son of God delights to take the Son of Man as a co-mate, and to bring flesh and blood even to the very gates of the Spiritual Kingdom. It would make the word Flesh, that it shall be seen and handled and felt.

Yes, dimmed as is the Divine Image in Man, it reflects not the full and fair Image of the Godhead. We seek it alone in Jesus in its fulness; yet sigh to behold it with our corporeal senses. And this privilege God ever vouchsafes to the pure and undefiled in heart; for he ever sends it upon the earth in the form of the Child. Herein have we a Type of the Divinity. Herein is our Nature yet despoiled of none of its glory. In flesh and blood he reveals his Presence to our senses, and pleads with us to worship and revere.

Childhood is yet a problem that we have scarce studied. But thus shall it not be always. It shall be apprehended. It shall not be a mystery and made to offend. "Light is springing up, and the dayspring from on high is again visiting us." And, as in times sacred to our associations, the Star led the Wise Men to the Infant Jesus, to present their reverent gifts, and was, at once, both the herald and the pledge of the advent of the Son of God on the earth; even so is the hour approaching and it lingers not on its errand, when the Wise and the Gifted, shall again surround the cradle of the New Born Babe, and there proffer, as did the Magi, their gifts of reverence and of love to the Holiness that hath visited the earth, and shines forth with a celestial glory around their heads;—and these, pondering well, as did Mary, the Divine Significance, shall steal from it the Art—so long lost in our Consciousness—of unfolding its powers into the fulness of the God.

And thus Man, repossessing his Idea, shall conform Nature to himself. Institutions shall bear the fruit of his regenerate being. They shall flourish in vigor and beauty. They shall circulate his Genius through Nature and Life, and repeat the story of his renewal.

Say not that this Era is distant. Verily, it is near. Even at this moment, the heralds of the time are announcing its approach. Omens of Good hover over us. A deeper and holier Faith is quickening the Genius of our Time. Humanity awaits the hour of its renewal. The renovating Fiat has gone forth, to revive our Institutions, and remould our Men. Faith is lifting her voice, and, like Jesus near the Tomb of Lazarus, is uttering the living words, "I am the Resurrection and the Life, and he that Believeth, though dead in doubts and sins, shall be reassured of his immortality, and shall flourish in unfading Youth! I will mould Nature and Man according to my Will. I will transfigure all things in the Image of my Ideal,"—And by such Faith, and such Vision, shall Education work its mission on the Earth. Apprehending the Divine Significance of Jesus—yet filled with the assurance of coming Messiahs to meet the growing nature of Man—shall inspired Genius go forth to renovate his Era; casting out the unclean spirits and the demons that yet afflict the Soul. And then shall Humanity, leaving her infirmities, her wrongs, her sufferings, and her sins, in the corrupting grave, reappear in the consciousness of Physical Purity; Inspired Genius; and spotless Holiness. Man shall be one with God, as was the Man of Nazareth.

Christian Science in Action

(The following letter to the *American Journal of Sociology* was written by the Manager of the Christian Science Committees on Publication and was published in the September, 1954, issue of that periodical. It is reprinted here in a somewhat abridged form.)

In your March issue R. W. E.—— examines five hundred "letters of testimony" in regard to Christian Science healing. These five hundred letters are presumably a representative selection from an extensive body of published evidence (amounting to many thousands of testimonials), largely neglected by social scientists.

It is gratifying to find an article paying serious attention to this evidence but a little surprising to note the polemic tone of some of the statements. More important, however, is Mr. E——'s method.

His key observation is based, as he says, "upon impressions rather than upon objective analysis." It has to do with the healing of diseases not to be classified as psychosomatic. He observes that the "number of cancers, tumors, broken bones, and cases of pneumonia and acute appendicitis which were self-diagnosed by the writers seemed large." Possibly so, though many Christian Scientists are particularly scrupulous in refraining from naming a disease that has not been medically diagnosed. But surely the crucial question for an investigator is: How many cases are there of healings of serious organic diseases that have been medically diagnosed? Mr. E—— simply sidesteps this question altogether.

The four volumes of *The Christian Science Journal* on which he based his investigation report the following healings in which there was medical diagnosis: four cases of cancer, eight of tumor, twenty-one of broken bones, seven of pneumonia, seven of appendicitis, twenty-two of heart disease, twenty-one of tuberculosis, six of asthma, and from one to three of diphtheria, blindness, peritonitis, scarlet fever, arthritis, spinal meningitis, diabetes, gallstones, epilepsy, tetanus, polio, uremic poisoning, pelvic ovaritis, smallpox, pyorrhea, hernia, deafness, curvature of the spine, jaundice, dropsy, bronchial catarrh, abscessed teeth, ulcerated eyes, paralytic stroke, etc.

This partial list, drawn from the data examined by Mr. E——, omits the large number of similar cases in which the context of the testimony implies medical diagnosis but does not explicitly state it. It leaves out such things as unspecified "growths" or "organic troubles" for which operations had previously been prescribed by physicians or unsuccessfully undertaken (in several cases repeatedly) and dubious cases, such as a knee condition diagnosed by one doctor as a tubercular joint and by another as a loose cartilage.

It does not include the more impressive features of the healings: their instantaneous nature in some instances (e.g., one of the cancer cases); the number which physicians or surgeons declared to be beyond remedying by operations or any other means, in several instances giving the patient only a few more hours or days to live; and the existence of such corroborative evidence as X-rays (showing for instance, in the case of a back broken in two places a perfect setting of the bones overnight without surgical aid—in fact, pronounced beyond surgical aid).

These testimonials, and thousands of similar ones, are on file at The Christian Science Publishing Society. As long ago as 1909, Benjamin O. Flower, editor of the mildly radical magazine, *The Arena*, published a book *(Christian Science as a Religious Belief and a Therapeutic Agent)* in which he included striking healings of organic disease by Christian Science based entirely on medical testimony. It is to be regretted that academic investigators have not pursued this more challenging line of inquiry instead of confining their attention to those cases which lend themselves to facile psychological explanations.

ii

(In the December 1954 issue of the *Minnesota Law Review* an article entitled "Criminal Liability in Faith Healing," by one C. C. Cawley, did the following things. It (1) lumped Christian Science together with "faith healing" of all varieties; (2) assumed that Christian Science cannot heal organic diseases and that medical science is infallible; (3) cited legal cases from the last century or early part of this century to prove that the provision of Christian Science treatment rather than medical treatment for a sick minor could be construed as "criminal neglect," but failed to mention the numerous legislative enactments which have subsequently provided that Christian Science treatment or treatment by prayer shall be considered as meeting the requirement for necessary medical care for a minor. Only a few months before, one of the regular weekly broadcasts of The Mother Church, in the radio series "How Christian Science Heals," had carried a testimony by a young woman of a healing which she had experienced in the very city in which the *Minnesota Law Review* is published. This testimony by Miss Lynn Whitney, now of Philadelphia, follows. It is worth noting that under Mr. Cawley's extraordinary thesis, Miss Whitney's parents would have been compelled to let her undergo an operation which she was given only one chance in a thousand of surviving.)

When I was thirteen years old I was suddenly stricken with a condition that caused my sinking, within a matter of hours, into a coma. I was unconscious for three days and nights. My mother, who was new in her study of Christian Science, but very earnest, called a Christian Science practitioner to pray for me when I became ill.

My father, who was not at that time a student of Christian Science, became frightened by the scene and insisted that I be removed at once to a hospital in Minneapolis, the city where we were then living. The resident doctor, who was very kindly and cooperative, agreed to my mother's request that because we were relying on prayer in Christian Science no medicine or injections were to be given me. Only the simplest, necessary nursing attention was to be provided.

In the meantime, my father engaged the services of three specialists in their respective fields who diagnosed my condition as tumor of the brain and spinal meningitis, both of which they informed my parents were fatal. One specialist, however, held out the hope that if a brain operation were performed at once I would have one chance in one thousand of surviving; but should this long chance not be taken, my passing would occur within a matter of hours.

At this point, when I was apparently dying, my mother informed the specialists there would be no operation; but that from now on the God she was coming to understand more and more through Christian Science as one of love would be wholly relied upon in this deep hour of human need. My father acquiesced to this decision and together they prayed the best they could, remembering the simple but healing words from a Christian Science hymn, "Trust the Eternal when the shadows gather"—and of course the practitioner was also praying. And within that hour, which had been told my parents would have seen my passing, there occurred instead an hour filled with victory and rejoicing, for I came out of the coma, recognized my parents and expressed my desire for food. In the matter of a week I left that hospital.

The resident doctor, so overcome with what he had witnessed, told my mother, with tears in his eyes, that he only wished he had known of this wonderful healing religion in time to have saved his young son who had succumbed to the same malady.

This healing was so complete and permanent that even the aftereffects of extreme weakness and speech paralysis which my parents had been told were inevitable were overcome within the month, and I again resumed my school activities.

Throughout the years that have followed, I have experienced many other remarkable healings through prayer as taught in Christian Science and have lived a wholly normal and active life both in the business world and in my present chosen profession of Christian Science nursing.

iii

(On Feb. 4, 1955, a testimony by Dr. Ernest H. Lyons, Jr., professor of chemistry at Principia College, Illinois, was presented on the regular weekly radio broadcast, "How Christian Science Heals." The relevant part of that broadcast follows.)

I was preparing a compound and I had to start with potassium cyanide. . . . To start the work I melted the potassium cyanide in an iron dish over a powerful burner. I set the iron stirring rod on the edge of the dish and turned away briefly. When I reached for the iron rod again I picked it up by the hot end. I dropped it immediately, but not before my hand was severely burned, and I could see crystals of the poison dislodged from the rod in the wound. But I was not frightened of poisoning for I was conscious of the presence of infinite Life, God, overruling the picture of accident and possible death. I washed my hand in water and wrapped it in a towel, and I was able to go ahead and complete the preparation. Within three days scarcely a scar remained and in less than a week all effects disappeared. Later I talked to an expert on cyanide poisoning and he told me that such an experience would ordinarily prove fatal in a few minutes.

(This testimony was later repeated on the television series of the same title. Following this telecast Dr. Lyons received a letter from a woman in California informing him that a consulting chemical engineer who roomed at her home had seen the program, had ridiculed the testimony as stating an evident impossibility, and had implied that the whole thing was fraudulent. The woman, who was a Christian Scientist, asked Dr. Lyons if he could give her a few facts that would indicate his standing as a chemist and a reliable witness. He replied by stating his professional background: B.S., Massachusetts Institute of Technology, 1931; M.S., California Institute of Technology, 1933; Chief Chemist, The Meaker Company, Chicago, Ill., 1934–46; Professor, Department of Chemistry, Principia College, 1946 to date; Ph.D., University of Illinois, 1953; Summer Lecturer in Chemistry, University of Illinois, 1955; author of numerous papers on electrodeposition and contributor to technical publications. In reply he received from his original critic the letter which follows.)

DEAR DR. LYONS:

Some weeks ago as I was watching the T.V. I saw the program conducted by the Christian Science church in which you appeared and gave a testimonial regarding a healing experience you once had with a burn from a hot, poisonous substance, potassium cyanide, as I recall. Mrs. ——, who is my landlady when I am in —— has been kind enuf to write you and has shown me your letter in reply. She did this because she is a devout Christian Scientist and was disturbed by my remarks about the unscientific nature of the evidence you presented.

Now it seems to me that as a chemist, you should be loath to give such testimony and make such statements as you did when you have no way of determining the amount of cyanide absorbed into your system at the time of the accident. Many of us in chemistry handle violent poisons, sometimes with our bare hands, and we do not suffer from them if we handle them intelligently. I do not need to remind you that H_2S is a violent poison, even rated above HCN, yet it is commonly used by chemists and even by students in analysis. I am sure you would not take a recognized lethal dose of cyanide by mouth or by injection and expect such a miraculous recovery.

Personally, I feel you have done the profession of chemistry a disservice by making the inaccurate and unverifiable statements you did. Such statements can be easily overlooked by us chemists but can have injurious effects on the layman who does not understand that chemical reactions proceed according to definite

laws and not according to the wishful thinking of the individual—
a fact that has taken our predecessors hundreds of years to
establish.

(In reply, Dr. Lyons wrote the letter which follows.)

DEAR MR. ———:

I can readily understand your reaction to my statements on the
TV program, because I questioned the incident myself until I
was forced to the conclusion which I presented there. Obviously,
it was impossible to give a detailed account on the program.

The accident occurred when I was preparing potassium cyan-
ate in order to carry out the Wohler synthesis of urea. The
wound, which extended across my right palm, exposed the ten-
dons. There appeared to be several masses of white crystals in the
fluids and burned tissues, but naturally I did not take time for an
extended inspection. The wound was so deep that for some days
my hand was drawn together.

There appear to be five possible explanations for my survival:

1. The material was not potassium cyanide. An old sample
might be completely hydrolyzed to the carbonate. In this event,
it would have been impossible to obtain urea. I obtained 10.8 g.,
whereas Coben's laboratory manual specifies 15 g. There is no
reason to expect decomposition of the cyanide on the stirring rod.

2. The shock, pain, and fright might have led me to imagine
crystals in the wound, or to mistake pieces of skin for crystals.
Since the end of the stirring rod was heavily coated with crystals,
it is virtually inconceivable that some were not dislodged and
entered the wound, whether I saw them or not. After the first
shock, I was surprisingly calm, and I doubt that hysteria influenced my observation.

3. The amount of potassium cyanide absorbed was below the
lethal level. This level is so low that such an occurance is highly
improbable. Furthermore, even a much smaller absorption leads
to milder symptoms, none of which were observed.

4. The cyanide was washed out of the wound without being
absorbed. In the opinion of a safety expert from duPont, sent to
check the safety practices of my former employers, who use

cyanide in ton lots, this is impossible under the circumstances described. A workman who fell into a relatively dilute cyanide solution in a plating machine my employers had installed in the Cadillac plant, was lifted promptly from the three foot deep tank, sprayed with a hose while his clothes were removed, and thoroughly washed until his death in about ten minutes, reportedly due to absorption of cyanide through the skin, although only the lower portions of his body were affected. This without a break in the skin.

5. Cyanide was absorbed but rendered harmless by the higher law of life. Although this may sound incredible, such instances are not uncommon to Christian Scientists. There is ample evidence, meeting both legal and scientific standards, that Christian Science healings have occurred which contravene material laws. In many instances, competent medical diagnoses were made before and afterwards.

The existence of a higher law, which can save life and relieve suffering in even the most hopeless circumstances, is so important that I am constrained to bring my experience to public notice. I cannot see that this will be any disservice to my profession; rather, the contrary.

As to taking another dose of cyanide, of course I would not do so voluntarily, nor would any other Christian Scientist. The reasoning on which this is based is explained in the Christian Science textbook. In reply to a similar question, Christ Jesus said, "It is written, thou shalt not tempt the Lord thy God." However, should I be exposed accidentally, my life could again be protected.

The exceedingly stringent demands made by Christian Science frequently lead me to examine and re-examine my reasons for accepting it, one of which is the experience recounted, but each time I have been forced to recognize that here is the science of sciences, the rational explanation of Jesus' healings, the answer to every need of humanity. I feel my protection was in direct fulfillment of Jesus' promise, "If they drink any deadly thing, it will not hurt them."

Very properly you will have your own interpretation of my experience, and it may not agree with mine. There is no need for controversy over this, but I hope that this account will show you that my statements are not based on wishful thinking, nor entirely unscientific evidence, nor unthinking enthusiasm, but in sincere acknowledgment of what seems to me to be the Christ.

Yours very truly,

ERNEST H. LYONS, JR.,

Head, Department of Chemistry

iv

(Because it is sometimes assumed that Christian Science is a "healing cult" with nothing to say to those who have no need of healing, the following testimony is included. It appeared in the *Christian Science Sentinel* of March 12, 1949, and was written by Sir James Butler, then Regius Professor of History at Cambridge University.)

. . . I have never had any spectacular physical healing; there has been no need, since I have enjoyed constant good health as long as I can remember. But I am grateful to Christian Science for help in innumerable ways throughout my school and college days, in the Army during both the wars, and in my university work. . . .

A little later came the exhilarating experience of class instruction from a teacher who enabled me to see more than ever before the grandeur and infinite range of Christian Science and the need to apply it to every circumstance. Later on I was present at the start of a Christian Science Organization at my university. This was nearly twenty years ago, and I can record what a great and beneficial part it has played in the careers of successive generations of students. I have also enjoyed the privilege of service in a branch church.

It has been my lot to live among intellectual people who have profound respect for the theories dominant among the foremost natural scientists and, while very tolerant of persons, are critical of methods of healing not accepted by the regular medical schools and of an intellectual outlook radically different from their own. I myself have a deep respect for the splendid qualities of mind and character shown by such leaders of human thought, but I cannot sufficiently express my gratitude for the blessing of having been taught in boyhood to distinguish as Mrs. Eddy does, between the human mind and the Mind which is God and to know that this Mind, combining infinite wisdom, power, and love, is, in Science, always expressing itself in perfect man and is, in human experience, constantly available to meet all our needs. "I can do all things through Christ which strengtheneth me" (Phil. 4:13). I am immensely grateful to our Leader, Mrs. Eddy, for revealing to us the Comforter promised by Christ Jesus and to her faithful followers for breaking for us this bread of Truth.

JAMES R. M. BUTLER
Cambridge, England

v

(With the growing emphasis on spiritual healing in the Protestant churches, it is sometimes stated that Christian Science has nothing to offer that cannot be found in traditional Christianity. A noted London physician, Dr. Christopher Woodard, who has elsewhere paid tribute to Christian Science and even acknowledged its part in the healing of his son, writes in *A Doctor's Faith Holds Fast:* "I can never understand why anyone professing Christian beliefs should find it helpful to seek guidance through . . . Christian Scientists . . . for surely that is a far less effective means of healing than the Divine way which we have been promised by Christ."

An excerpt from an authorized lecture on Christian Science as printed in the *Townsman* (Wellesley, Massachusetts) on May 31, 1956, is relevant to this comment. The lecture was delivered by Friedrich Preller, of Berlin, Germany, a courageous anti-Nazi who was arrested by the Nazis and imprisoned for a time during World War II, and who later became a teacher of Christian Science. The experience Mr. Preller relates is his own, though given in the third person. In delivering this lecture, Mr. Preller has customarily explained to his audience that "the boy who was healed is the man who is speaking to you today.")

A young man learned of Christian Science when he was nineteen years of age. Up to that time he had prayed a great deal in the way he had been taught as a child. Within a few years he lost his mother, his father, and his brother. Due to an accident, he himself suffered a serious hip disease, and doctors had declared his case incurable. Because of the death of his mother he leaned more than ever on God for loving care, and in so doing his prayers underwent a change. He now prayed as his heart dictated, and he felt happier. His prayers, evidencing a firm faith, made it easier for him to bear his loss and his physical suffering. He was confined to a hospital for fifteen months. He bore all his sorrow with a certain dignity, believing that God had ordained this experience of suffering for him. The last time he was in the hospital the New Testament was his only literature. Not only did he read a chapter from the Gospels each day—he studied it. He was disconcerted as he discovered a difference between the Biblical record and the sermons preached from the pulpit. One day he was discharged as incurable and, in order to walk at all, was obliged to wear an orthopedic brace. His right leg was two inches shorter than his left leg. He continued to attend church, but the conflict regarding his faith increased, and very soon he was led to withdraw entirely from the church. But his communion with God increased, and his prayers were now a sincere desire for right guidance. Undoubtedly the change was brought about through his prayer expressed in the words of the Psalmist (139: 23, 24): "Search me, O God, and know my heart: try me, and know my thoughts: and see if there be any wicked way in me, and lead me in the way everlasting."

When, two weeks after the young man's withdrawal from the church, he learned of Christian Science, he felt without question that his prayer had been heard. He became acquainted with a Christian Scientist who, at his request, explained a few fundamental truths regarding this, to him, new religion. She told him in particular what Christian Science teaches about God, man, and man's unity with God. When he was alone again, he let these few but mighty thoughts do their work in his consciousness. Suddenly it was as though scales fell from his eyes. What he had sought in prayer, sensed and felt through an earnest study of the Bible, but had expected only beyond the grave, became a present experience through that first contact with Christian Science. Complete newness of life with undreamed-of possibilities unfolded for him. He felt at home at once in the atmosphere of this religion. With a quickening of thought which made the physical become of no significance to him, he grasped for the first time what it means to be the child of God and thus be able to enjoy God's love, goodness, and presence. He was so preoccupied with rightly cherishing in thought his newly acquired understanding that when he went to bed and removed the brace from his body, he did not think at all of a physical healing. When he awakened the next morning, he discovered that for the first time in five and one half years he could stand and walk without pain. About two weeks later his right leg had regained its normal length and strength.

Why was it that this healing did not come to the young man until Christian Science had touched his consciousness, although there had previously been such strong faith and fervent prayer? Undoubtedly it was because his ignorance of God, that is, the belief that illness was in accordance with God's will, had prevented such a demonstration. But now the seed of Christian Science had fallen on prepared soil. A suddenly illuminated understanding of God, accompanied by deep joy, had made prayer capable of bringing results. This experience comprised three essential points of the Christian Scientist's faith: the influx of the divine Spirit, the birth of the Christ in human consciousness, and the resurrection to a new life.

BIBLIOGRAPHICAL
NOTE

In addition to the books mentioned in the text and footnotes, a few other works should be listed for their relevance or usefulness. *The Transcendentalists,* edited by Perry Miller (Cambridge, Harvard University Press, 1950), is an invaluable anthology of Transcendentalist writings for the general reader. Harold C. Goddard's *Studies in New England Transcendentalism* (New York, Lemcke & Buechner, 1908) supplements the classic history by Frothingham. *The Orient in American Transcendentalism,* by Arthur Christy (New York, Columbia University Press, 1932) covers a particularly significant aspect of the subject. *The Life of Ralph Waldo Emerson,* by Ralph L. Rusk (New York, Charles Scribner's Sons, 1949) is the most comprehensive and authoritative portrait of the leader of the Concord group, but *Freedom and Fate,* by Stephen E. Whicher (Philadelphia, University of Pennsylvania Press, 1953), penetrates most percipiently to the central spiritual dilemma of Emerson, as suggested in this book.

Pedlar's Progress: The Life of Bronson Alcott, by Odell Shepard (Boston, Little, Brown & Co., 1937), is the definitive biography of the Schoolmaster of Transcendentalism, though the older two-volume work by Sanborn and Harris, *A. Bronson Alcott: His Life and Philosophy* (Boston, Little, Brown & Co., 1893), still contains the most satisfactory account of his philosophical thinking. *The Journals of Bronson Alcott,* edited by Odell Shepard (Boston, Little, Brown & Co., 1938), are of course indispensable and include the references to Mrs. Eddy which are quoted in the present book. The Alcott-Eddy friendship has received scant attention from writers. A short chapter is devoted to it in *Mary Baker Eddy, the Truth and the Tradition,* by Bates and Dittemore (New York, Alfred A. Knopf, 1932), but these writers show a tendency here, as elsewhere in their book, to select only

229

such parts of the correspondence as will support their thesis. Woodbridge Riley's contribution to *The Faith, the Falsity, and the Failure of Christian Science* (New York, Fleming H. Revell, 1925) claims an intellectual "influence" of Alcott on Mrs. Eddy, but is of so sketchy and polemic a character as to suggest a superficial approach to the thought of both.

The best introduction to Mrs. Eddy is through her own works. Of the many biographies and memoirs of her available, no single volume does full justice to so many-faceted a character. In contrast to the number and diversity of biographies, there is a dearth of published material on the later history of Christian Science. *Historical Sketches* by Clifford P. Smith (Boston, The Christian Science Publishing Society, 1941), contains useful documentation for the earlier period and includes some account of the spread of Christian Science to Great Britain and Germany. *The Continuing Spirit*, by Norman Beasley (New York, Duell, Sloan and Pearce, 1956), is a popular history of the Church since 1910, written by an admiring outsider. The chapter on Christian Science contributed by Arthur J. Todd to *Religion in the Twentieth Century* (New York, Philosophical Library, 1948) is a useful summing up by a Christian Scientist who was also a highly regarded sociologist. *Commitment to Freedom, The Story of The Christian Science Monitor*, by Erwin D. Canham (Boston, Houghton Mifflin Co., in press) is a comprehensive history covering the fifty-year existence of the paper.

INDEX